ORDINARY
MIRACLES

ORDINARY
MIRACLES

MOLLY HAWKINS

authorHOUSE®

AuthorHouse™
1663 Liberty Drive
Bloomington, IN 47403
www.authorhouse.com
Phone: 1-800-839-8640

© 2013 by Molly Hawkins. All rights reserved.

No part of this book may be reproduced, stored in a retrieval system, or transmitted by any means without the written permission of the author.

Published by AuthorHouse   02/25/2013

ISBN: 978-1-4817-8110-7 (sc)
ISBN: 978-1-4817-8111-4 (e)

This book is printed on acid-free paper.

Because of the dynamic nature of the Internet, any web addresses or links contained in this book may have changed since publication and may no longer be valid. The views expressed in this work are solely those of the author and do not necessarily reflect the views of the publisher, and the publisher hereby disclaims any responsibility for them.

Contents

Acknowledgments vii
Foreword..ix
Introduction..xiii
Prologue...xv

Chapter One	An Amazing Place	1
Chapter Two	Experiencing The Impossible	19
Chapter Three	A New Life Begins	30
Chapter Four	Every Day Something New	42
Chapter Five	In Everything Give Thanks!	56
Chapter Six	Healings And Hauntings	72
Chapter Seven	Dreams And Disaster	91
Chapter Eight	Hallelujah Anyway!	103
Chapter Nine	"Trust In The Lord . . ."	114
Chapter Ten	You Must Be Joking!	131
Chapter Eleven	Not Quite Fawlty Towers!	150
Chapter Twelve	Time To Say Goodbye	168

Acknowledgments

My grateful thanks to our sons and their families for their love and encouragement, and especially to Simon and Andrew for their patient and detailed editing. My thanks too, to our friend John Newth for his generous Foreword, and to all who contributed to the telling of this story.

Above all, I give thanks to Almighty God, without whose help and inspiration this book would never have been written.

I dedicate 'Ordinary Miracles' to the precious memory of Norman, beloved husband, father and grandfather.

FOREWORD

IT IS QUITE unusual to make new deep friendships when one is middle aged. However when my wife Elizabeth, daughter Keren and I met Molly Hawkins and her late husband Norman nearly 30 years ago, we immediately bonded into a friendship that continues to this day. In some ways our lives have been similar, particularly as we both left a mainstream Christian denomination and commenced meetings in our respective homes. Norman and Molly ministered at our fellowship in Eastbourne on one occasion.

Molly's book illustrates three of her many attributes. One is her loving attitude to individuals whether or not they are yet Christian believers. Another is the fact that she is a modest and honest person who identifies with ordinary people, despite the fact that, with God, she and Norman have achieved extraordinary things. The third vital characteristic is that Molly has a healthy non-religious sense of humour.

The section of the book on South Chard is interesting and illuminating. Our family didn't have the opportunity to visit during the 'glory years', but we came to know some of the leading characters later on, and were able to visit the church in the 1980s. The description of events at Chard are an important pen picture of one of the pioneering works of the Holy Spirit in the 1960s and 1970s which became part of what was known as the charismatic movement.

We stayed at Babbacombe Villa Hotel on numerous occasions and our Fellowship also had a holiday there. Our perceptions as guests were good. The hotel was light and airy and the food excellent.

Meeting new people of various temperaments, views and Christian perspectives contrasted with the absence of 'canned' entertainment. Each evening after the meal, guests tended to congregate in the lounge and interesting conversations took place as new friends were made.

The short and voluntary Bible studies before breakfast were sometimes led by one of the guests. One was Hugh Black, a retired headmaster from Scotland and leader of the 'Struthers' movement. He was invited back to lead a weekend conference at the hotel, also attended by a number of regular guests and some local people. David & Denise Critchell came to the hotel considering full-time Christian service. Denise is now a Church of England vicar, and she and David work full-time in Christian work in the Buckinghamshire area.

Babbacombe Villa was no commercial, money-making enterprise, but a loving service to its guests. Care, love and compassion for individuals, initially in their home meetings, then at Chard and in their travelling ministry, followed by the Babbacombe Villa venture, were the characteristics that typified Norman and Molly. Their ministries have touched many lives.

Molly titles her book 'Ordinary Miracles', but it could more aptly be entitled 'Extraordinary Miracles'. I believe that in these days when apathy and cynicism permeate our society, as well as elements of the church, this book will be an inspiration and challenge to all who read it.

John Newth—Eastbourne

INTRODUCTION

TRAVELLING ALONG THE North Circular Road from our home in North London on our way to our destination, the little village of South Chard in Somerset, I was conscious of a sense of almost unbearable excitement. It was a beautiful Whit Saturday in May 1968, and my husband Norman and I, together with our three young sons, were on our way to a Full Gospel Church which we had heard about through a young woman working in Norman's Careers Office at The Barbican, London.

Her name was Fiona Blaikley, and she told us of a gathering of people there who really believed the Bible. They and many visitors from all over the world were experiencing miracles of healing and deliverance, worship and praise which in the formal Methodist Churches which we had attended for 25 years was then unknown.

For so long we had looked around at folk in the pews, so many needs and problems—a mother whose rebellious son was in deep trouble, another almost suicidal, grieving families with constant sickness, and so on, wondering where the signs and wonders of the Acts of the Apostles were—why did we never see them today, when the Bible tells us God is the same, yesterday, today and forever? (Heb 13:8)

We had been told for so long that these events were only for that time, but might it be possible that God really was working in His Church in a truly dynamic way *now?* Well, if so we wanted to be there to see it for ourselves, so here we were motoring along the A30 towards Chard on this glorious sunny Whit Saturday morning.

As I watched soft white clouds scudding across a vivid blue sky I remembered how many times I had longed to be amongst them—perhaps up there I could feel nearer to God. But this time I *knew* without a shadow of doubt that at last we were about to meet Him in a far deeper way . . .

Prologue

This book began long before the Lord called my beloved husband Norman home and I felt compelled to continue to share our story. It spans a period of over 50 years, so I have only touched on particular events that I hope you will find encouraging. For the sake of privacy names have sometimes been changed.

Many Christians long to move in the power of God—and may not always realise that although we all receive the Holy Spirit when we are born again, He empowers us to move in His gifts even more so when we are baptized (filled, immersed) in this same Spirit.

Some feel defeated, others frustrated, discouraged or despairing as they see those sometimes described as "mighty men and women of faith" moving in power and miracles. They find it difficult to believe God could ever work through *them*, ordinary men and women like ourselves who long to experience the power and presence of God in a much more dynamic way.

My husband and I have experienced so many wonderful and extraordinary touches from the Lord, despite all our mistakes. At times I have almost lost my faith and we have been through some very deep waters—yet God in His love and mercy through Jesus Christ has always picked us up, dusted us down and encouraged us to persevere.

Even though there are times when, no matter how firm our faith, our prayers appear to be unanswered, my hope is that the events recorded in this book may help readers believe that miracles *are* possible—especially if we have the courage to trust the Word of God and *learn how to pray with the authority we have been given.* (Eph 6:10-18) King James Version

Do remember that in between wonderful happenings, our life was as mundane as everyone else's—we had our ups and downs, excitements and disappointments—but with Jesus Christ always at the centre.

I am chronicling the good and bad, for often, though the mountaintop experience is wonderful and exhilarating, it is in the valleys that the Lord reveals Himself to us and we truly know Him as our Comforter and Friend who never fails us.

Molly Hawkins

CHAPTER ONE

AN AMAZING PLACE

When Fiona Blaikley joined my husband Norman and his staff at the London Barbican Careers office, little did we know what an enormous impact she would make. Young and single, she was a pleasant and conscientious worker who blended well with her colleagues.

It was unusual for someone to read the Bible in the office, and when she did so during her lunch break this drew the attention of George. Now George was very much a staid bachelor of whom it was said, rather unkindly, by another colleague that the most exciting thing he ever did was polish his shoes every night! But no one could have guessed how dramatically his life would change over the next few weeks.

He was obviously intrigued by Fiona's strong faith, particularly when she came back from a weekend away at a Full Gospel church in a little Somerset village called South Chard, near Ilminster. She apologised for her greasy hair, explaining that she had needed prayer for healing and the elders at the Church had been a bit over-generous with the anointing oil!

This was new to us all, and George began to question Fiona about what were to him her strange beliefs. She explained that anointing with oil for healing was described in the Bible and showed him the book of James in the New Testament (James 5: 14,15) He then admitted to being an agnostic but with a real longing to know God, so she gently suggested that he kneel by his bedside later and simply ask the Lord to forgive him for past sins and make Himself real to him.

George told us later that he had gone home and done precisely that but had eventually fallen asleep very disappointed (though not at all surprised) that nothing happened. However, in the middle of the night he awoke to hear his name called . . . "George!" He jumped up with such a start he hit the headboard with a resounding thwack, and rubbing the lump on his head felt confused but certain of what he had heard.

Shortly afterwards the voice spoke again—louder—and by now,of course, he was thoroughly awake . . . *"GEORGE!"* This time he knew with utter certainty that God had spoken to him and that He *was* real after all! We don't know exactly what followed; only that this experience changed his life completely.

The next morning he walked into Norman's office, radiant and with a huge smile, exclaiming, "I've got something really important to tell you!" Norman took one look at him, knew it had to be something extraordinarily good, and was amazed and delighted when George confessed that God had spoken to him the previous night and he had become a Christian—truly born again, just as Jesus describes in John 3.3.

His office colleagues, and doubtless his friends, too, couldn't help but see the remarkable change in him. Gone was his stuffy correctness; he radiated profound warmth and love, a new and tremendous zest for life and a longing to know more about the Lord Jesus. The Bible and its relevance to the present day fascinated him, and after he died his friends told us that he had spent the remainder of his life telling others about his Lord and seeing lives changed.

Fiona confessed to Norman years later that when she was sent to the Barbican office by her Agency it was the very last place she had wanted to go to. The Barbican was an awkward journey from her home and she was looking for work locally, but at the time that office had the only suitable vacancy. Little did she know then what an incredibly life-changing influence her presence would have on us all!

When Norman told me what was happening at the Church in South Chard I knew at last that this was where I should be baptised. God had been speaking to me for many months about my need for water baptism by immersion, but I knew instinctively that, although they were lovely people, for some unknown reason the local Baptist Church wasn't the right place. Our Methodist church didn't believe water baptism was necessary anyway, so I just waited to see what the Lord wanted.

Now, however, after hearing about the wonderful things happening at South Chard—healing, deliverance, and the gifts of the Holy Spirit in evidence—I was convinced that this was where I needed to be. Norman was just as intrigued as I was by it all. So . . . here we were on our journey along the A30 towards the West Country.

We were all excited for different reasons; Norman and I because we knew there was a very special spiritual experience ahead of us, and our three sons (Duncan, aged 11, Simon 8 and Andrew 4) were looking forward to holidaying in Somerset for the first time. We knew we would be staying with Fiona and her two friends in her bungalow in Chard, and that everyone in the Church called the Pastor Uncle Sid and his wife Auntie Mill.

Their home was called The Manor House (originally three modest thatched cottages joined together) next to the Church—which had originally been a barn, and which Sid Purse, in those days a farmer, had himself with help built into a place of worship. Eventually, when numbers increased dramatically, a balcony was installed.

We were told people came from far and wide, not only from all over the UK but many places worldwide, usually staying as guests in the homes of Church members. Those who came were hungry for teaching and ministry and deeply touched when they experienced the depth of praise and worship. The more we heard about what happened at this Church, the more we longed to see for ourselves.

We had visited Chard a few times when the Purses explained that they originally belonged to the Brethren, but had received the Baptism of the Holy Spirit through the ministry of a missionary when she visited them at their home in the early 1950s. This had changed their lives dramatically, and that was when the Lord began to speak to them about building a church in their barn. When it was completed, people began to be drawn there in increasing numbers.

God also spoke to Uncle Sid very clearly about taking away the beautiful pulpit, which according to Auntie Mill, a member of the congregation had taken great pains to construct and carve. Apparently this decision didn't go down too well with certain members of the congregation (who promptly left!), but as Uncle Sid studied the Scriptures he became more and more convinced that God was showing him that only the Holy Spirit, and *not* man, should lead the meetings.

Gradually Body Ministry came into being, with everyone encouraged to use their spiritual gifts. Uncle Sid was a small man in stature but with a mighty ministry of deliverance, and I remember being in his pegboard-lined vestry one day asking how it was that he was never hurt when we knew people asking him for help could occasionally be extremely violent as they were being prayed for.

He smiled, and said in his soft Somerset accent: "Molly, I'm covered in the precious blood of Jesus. Look at that . . ." He pointed to a large dent in the pegboard. "One man was very angry, full of rage. He actually tried to punch *me* too, but he could get no further than a few inches away from my face! I know I am covered and protected by the blood of Jesus!" In chapter 9 verse 1 of Luke's Gospel we are told God has given us authority over *all* the power of the enemy, and as God's child and full of faith, this man could not touch Uncle Sid.

All of our sons love music, and Simon, who played by ear, often played the organ in the church services from when he was only twelve and loved to practice there on his own. Uncle Sid told us of one man who was telling him his troubles in the vestry. He was very angry and resentful at life in general. In the middle of a tirade he suddenly stopped and listened. "Who's playing the organ?" he asked gruffly. "Go and have a look!" suggested Uncle Sid. When the man saw young Simon with his eyes closed, silently worshipping the Lord through his music, he broke down. His heart was touched and he was then open to ministry.

As time went on a number of men in the church felt they should meet and pray together every morning before work, and after some months as a direct consequence we were told that people coming to the church during the 1960s were sometimes so convicted by the power of God they would be overcome and be unable to stand, not only as they walked through the doors, but even as they crossed the car park!

Newcomers would hear God speaking directly to them as they sat in the services through visions or prophecy, and this is something we greatly miss when a church doesn't use these wonderful gifts of the Holy Spirit. Many times it is a great blessing to hear the Lord speaking words of comfort and encouragement to us through total strangers.

Our first experience of this was during our second visit to the church. I had walked across the empty car park to a bungalow in the church grounds (called The Miracle!) where we were staying. I always felt I walked with two left feet, and on this occasion was just as embarrassed as usual, crossing the car park wishing I was invisible even though there was absolutely no one else around.

You can imagine my astonishment when in the middle of that evening's service a late visitor who was a complete stranger stood and prophesied: "My child, why do you stoop and stare at the ground when you walk? Don't you know you are the child of a King? Lift up your head and keep your eyes on Me as you walk in the path I have ordained for you, for I love you, saith the Lord." It wasn't until about three weeks later that I realised I no longer had a problem walking across open spaces!

A few years after we moved to Chard a lady called Margaret Godfree, who had a proven prophetic ministry, suddenly stood in the middle of a meeting and began to prophesy (Incidentally, prophecy does not necessarily mean foretelling the future, but it is the Word of the Lord in season—for encouragement, comfort and edification, as Scripture says in 1 Corinthians 14:3).

"My son, I am *not* the God of a duck!" she began. We all looked at each other in some consternation, wondering if she had suddenly lost the plot! But Margaret, who knew nothing whatsoever about cricket, described certain facets of the game as she went on to tell one particular young man, who loved and played cricket, that God was on his (winning!) side, that he was not to be dismayed but to know that whatever happened God was helping and supporting him.

By the end of the prophecy that young man was in tears, and afterwards it transpired that he had been going through a particularly difficult time and crisis of faith, really needing to know God was there and loved him. Margaret, meanwhile, had no idea who the Lord was speaking to, or of the teenager's problems.

Many times when we really needed assurance and help when going through one of the deep valleys we all experience I would ask God fervently for a word from Him—and He never disappointed us.

For instance, some years later, after we had moved to Babbacombe, Torquay, we found ourselves in a very difficult financial situation. This was directly linked to what happened as we sought to dispose of the hotel we had been running which led to some significant unexpected expenses.

After eventually selling the hotel we were left with almost no savings but needed to plan some improvements to the new property, which would enable us to open our home for bed and breakfast guests to help bring in an additional income. After seven years of financial struggle the task of steadying our household finances seemed impossible, no matter how hard we worked. By then I was in a state of constant anxiety because of what seemed our sheer helplessness.

Then one day while Norman was travelling midweek as a publishers' representative away from home I decided to attend a revival meeting in a local Anglican church; I was in an agony of mind, desperately needing the Lord's encouragement and comfort.

Sitting next to me were a couple I had never met before, but a few minutes after the service began the wife turned to me and said "The Lord has given me a word for you. I see you standing on a mountaintop but the wind is very, very cold. You have experienced these bitter winds for a long time, but as I watched the dark clouds went away and you were standing under a beautiful blue sky. God says that from now on the south winds will blow upon you and . . . 'as you trust in Me, saith the Lord, I will help you. And I *will* use you, for you are not worthless, you are <u>not</u> worthless, for I have a ministry waiting for you. So do not fear, but believe My word, knowing you are safe in My hands, saith the Lord.'"

There was no way this dear lady could have known of our plight, or of the fact that I had thought sadly for some time that it seemed I was of no more use in ministry. You can imagine my astonishment when I discovered she and her husband had been in far deeper debt than we had been during their bed and breakfast business years, and that when at last they surrendered the whole situation to the Lord He had, over time, set them completely free.

What an encouragement this was; such a sense of enormous relief simply knowing our Heavenly Father was in charge and would rescue us. I couldn't wait to share the news with Norman when he arrived home later that evening from his travels. And, for the first time, we had the courage to relinquish our situation totally; prepared to go bankrupt if necessary if that was what the Lord had in mind for us.

Thanks to our son Andrew's help, too, with skilful negotiations with our creditors, the Lord Jesus was true to His Word and *did* wonderfully deliver us from the brink of bankruptcy. Knowing we were out of debt at last filled us with huge relief and gratitude.

The enemy of our souls will try to counterfeit these gifts of the Spirit through fortune-telling and other occult practices and as a result many Christians have been robbed of the Holy Spirit's blessing through fear of the supernatural, but Satan can never counterfeit the love of God. It is this same wonderful love that wants us to hear His voice speaking directly to us through such gifts.

However, going back to that very first evening visit to the Church over Whitsun in 1968, we arrived in time for tea with Fiona and her friends, and although the Saturday evening service didn't begin until six thirty we were told we needed to be there by at least six o'clock to find seats where we could all see what was happening. When we took our places just before six we could only find room for the eight of us in the balcony, but from the front seats we had a perfect view and a short while later even the balcony was full.

We were amazed at the number of children and young people who, together with the adults, seemed almost on tiptoes with excitement and anticipation waiting for the service to begin. Many had tambourines. On this beautiful summer evening the sun illuminated the texts scrolled on the walls. Over the baptistry platform and in the centre of the wall was the Scripture "Ye shall know the Truth, and the Truth shall make you free". (John 8:32) As time went on this proved to be so true in our own experience.

Our three boys sat riveted. Only the previous Sunday Duncan had protested that he didn't want to go to Sunday School any more as he found it pointless and boring—and since it was meant to be a happy experience we weren't sure how best to encourage him.

Sitting on this balcony, though, we were all aware of how totally different this church was; the presence of the Holy Spirit so real and tangible, unlike anything we had ever experienced before, and not a spare seat in the place. My overwhelming emotion was one of yearning, hunger for what all these Christians were enjoying—the infilling of the precious Holy Spirit.

The anticipation heightened until, at around half past six, without any announcement or warning, the organist suddenly began to play a chorus with great gusto and the whole place erupted joyously, tambourines playing with great enthusiasm and skill. We were amazed to see children and adults dancing, praising the Lord with great joy, their faces radiant. I felt tears pricking the back of my eyes. "This is what dancing is *really* for", I thought, remembering the many times Norman and I had enjoyed ballroom dancing together.

There were no hymn books (although we discovered later that they occasionally used Redemption Hymnal), but the choruses they sang were simple to remember and we sang them over and over again—another new experience. Most were neither hymns nor songs exactly, but rather something in between. They were very compelling. Some were composed by a gifted young singer and songwriter, a member of the

Church called Andrew Culverwell whose music was clearly anointed, and who later moved to the United States with his wife and family to further his songwriting career.

We soon came to realise that there were a number of gifted musicians in the congregation playing the organ and piano, though I remember thinking at first: "Why do they all have to keep singing the same words over and over again; surely they must know them well enough by now!" However, as we learned how to truly praise and worship the Lord with all our heart, soul, mind and spirit we realised that it wasn't until we had sung a chorus for perhaps the sixth or seventh time that the words (often straight from Scripture) became truly alive within us, building and cementing our faith.

So many things happened that evening that were completely new to us. As I have already described, there was no pulpit on the baptistry platform, but instead at least 30 children of all ages sitting on several rows of chairs. We were amazed to see those as young as five or six years old with their arms raised and eyes closed, worshipping the Lord. There didn't appear to be any particular leader. Apparently Uncle Sid, the Pastor, always sat in the congregation since he believed the service should be led wholly by the Holy Spirit, and indeed there was great expectation, never knowing quite what would happen next.

He also believed in Body Ministry—that anyone should be free to take an active part; perhaps to share a Scripture and teach on it, or give a word of knowledge or prophecy—in other words, that the gifts of the Holy Spirit should be in operation. He had tremendous trust in the Lord that everything would be done "decently and in order . . ."(1

Cor.14: 39,40) and if someone occasionally over the years tried to teach a wrong (unscriptural) doctrine, it was corrected very sensitively, so as not to embarrass that person or discourage others from sharing.

At about eight o'clock the platform was cleared, the baptistry opened, and to our astonishment a total of 27 people were baptised that night. We would never forget the joyous singing (and dancing!) after each baptism. Long before the end of the evening Norman and I knew we should follow suit, but weren't sure whether Fiona would mind if the five of us stayed until Monday morning.

At the end of this incredible day, when the boys were in bed and we were drinking our cocoa, we hesitantly asked if it would be possible to stay one more night. To our great relief Fiona and her friends were overjoyed, particularly when they knew we were going to be baptised the following day. We were so grateful. We knew this was to be a real turning point in our lives.

Our time on that Sunday included prayer and preparation for the evening service, and this time we all sat downstairs near the baptistry. I'd always imagined we'd need white robes, but the men wore a shirt and trousers, the women a one-size-fits-all kind of dress from the dozens in the airing cupboard in the vestry. This time there were no fewer than *29* of us queuing to give our testimony before going into the water—and baptism was never taken lightly. Uncle Sid taught that the Church didn't go in for 'sheep dipping', but those taking part always had to know the true meaning of baptism.

We were each invited to give our testimony, and once we had stepped down into the pool we stood with our hands crossed over our chest, two strong deacons waiting to give time for the Lord to speak to each individual, either through Scripture or prophecy or perhaps a vision, before baptising us.

Neil Porthouse, Fiona's boyfriend whom we met that evening, had an encouraging word of prophecy as I stood in the baptismal pool. Immediately afterwards someone gave another prophecy, full of warmth, assuring me of God's love, which I found very moving. Then, on confession of my faith, my old self was 'buried' in the waters of baptism in the Name of the Lord Jesus Christ, to be raised up in new life in Him (Romans 6:4) and Norman was next to give his testimony and be baptized.

It was one of the most wonderful experiences of our lives; we felt totally cleansed, as white as snow inwardly as well as outwardly, and very conscious of the nearness of our wonderful Lord Jesus. We realised we had a very long way to go and wouldn't be anywhere near perfect until we got to Heaven, but this had to be a big step in the right direction!

Afterwards, as I finished dressing in the vestry, the organist, Pam Greenwood, wife of Harry, who had a ministry of healing, came into the room and asked if I would like to be filled with the Holy Spirit. I couldn't wait! She placed her hands gently on my head, praying quietly in a strange language, and encouraging me to speak out any unfamiliar words or syllables in my mind.

After a few moments one or two unexpected syllables popped into my thoughts, beginning with "abba, abba . . ." It was only a very long time later that I realised I had been saying "Father" or "Daddy"—especially comforting since my parents had divorced when I was 8 years old and I really missed a relationship with my Dad. (At first we both had only a syllable or two at a time, which we kept practising until the language began to flow!) I wondered how Pam had known I longed for this gift of the Holy Spirit since we had never met before, but later we came to understand 'words of knowledge' (1 Corinthians 12:8)

In the meantime, while Pam was praying for me, Norman was in another little room where several deacons had gathered around praying for him to receive the gift of tongues. He said afterwards he told them he had read about John Wesley's heart being "strangely warmed", and would like a similar experience, please! Suddenly Uncle Sid appeared in the doorway, asking if there was a problem.

"Norman wants to be baptised in the Spirit but nothing seems to be happening", was the reply.

"Norman, have you had anything to do with Freemasonry?" Uncle Sid spoke with authority.

"No".

"Or Jehovah's Witnesses?"

"No".

"Or the occult in any way?"

"No".

"Then receive the Holy Spirit!" he exclaimed, laying his hands on Norman. This time he began immediately to speak in another heavenly language! When we returned to the service we were *both* on cloud nine because now the presence of Jesus was so real, and we felt His love so strongly.

As staid Methodists it was unheard of to raise our hands during a service, but now we both felt we just couldn't keep our hands in our laps—we felt compelled to raise them in worship as we sang and praised the Lord. It was wonderful; He was gently setting us free.

One of my most memorable experiences was grasping what had happened while I had been standing in the waters of baptism. Enjoying our hot chocolate back at the bungalow I thanked Neil warmly for the words of encouragement he had given.

"By the way, who was the man who gave the second prophecy immediately afterwards?" I asked.

They all looked at each other, obviously puzzled, and asked what I meant.

"You know, just after Neil spoke. There was this lovely prophecy, all about the love of God?"

But no one else had heard those clearly spoken words—and it was only then that I realised it must have been the Lord Jesus Himself speaking to me. I had a sense of awe and deep gratitude.

We awoke the next morning with great joy to what we knew was a brand-new start and an excitement that we had begun a voyage of discovery of the gifts and fruits of the Spirit—there was so much we longed to learn about our deeper walk with Jesus. There was just an inner conviction for us both, too, that the Lord was changing our whole outlook on many things. We were so hungry to learn more, and to be available for whatever the Lord wanted; we owed Him so much.

Only three years later each of our sons came to us individually, asking to be baptised and fully understanding their need for water baptism. That too, was a very memorable and joyous time and we have kept and cherished the words of prophecy each was given—all of which have been or are being fulfilled.

At the time we had no idea how vital this whole experience would be. The gift of tongues (speaking in a new language given us by God) has proved to be invaluable, and we soon discovered that one of the prime reasons for the use of any of the gifts is to bless and help others.

For instance, some years ago while laying hands on a lady longing for this infilling she began to speak in Latin, starting with Te Deum (which we discovered later means "Praise God!"). We knew just enough to recognise the language.

After a few minutes we asked her if she knew what language she was speaking. When she replied that she had no idea, we explained that it was Latin and she burst into tears. "My husband thinks tongues are just gobbledygook hysteria!" she said, "and it's the only foreign language he knows!

When I go home I'll speak to him in my new tongue and he can translate for me! He must believe now!" What a loving miracle she was given!

A friend, Gillian Davies, shared with us how she was at a prayer meeting where among those taking part was a woman who was studying linguistics, knew many languages, and was very skeptical of speaking in tongues. However, after a period of praise in tongues (it sounds like glorious angelic singing which begins and ends as though a Divine Conductor is leading) Gillian opened her eyes and saw this woman staring at her in disbelief.

"Where did you learn to speak Russian?" she asked. Gillian replied that she didn't know the language and had never spoken it.

"Oh yes, you did", was the reply. "You have just sung the Lord's Prayer in fluent Russian!"

Norman, too, spoke aloud in tongues at a meeting where There were many Swedish visitors. He didn't speak Swedish at all, but afterwards several of them thanked him for his timely message in their native language!

There are many instances where God uses this gift to benefit others just at the time it is most needed. During that brief weekend at South Chard we saw people healed and set free from all kinds of oppression, and during the years that followed we were to experience many other miracles. We would have been amazed if we had known then what God was planning to do in our own lives.

Chapter Two
EXPERIENCING THE IMPOSSIBLE . . .

When we returned home to Oakwood, North London and to our Methodist Church, two of our closest friends, John and Doreen Badkin, took one look at us and asked what had happened. We were completely unaware, but it was apparently obvious that we had changed; we certainly felt great peace and joy. We briefly described our experiences over the past weekend and they immediately said they, too, would like to visit South Chard; they were as hungry spiritually as we had been.

In the meantime Norman continued to lead the Young People's Fellowship at our local Methodist Church back in North London where Duncan was persuaded to continue attending Sunday School for the time being. A few days later John asked if we would share our experiences with a number of folk he was inviting from the Methodist Church. We were very happy to do so, and a few days later found ourselves in John's comfortable sitting room describing everything that had happened to us. In the middle of it all Doreen suddenly jumped up and ran out of the room, telling us afterwards that the presence of Jesus was so real she was afraid she might see Him if she stayed!

We were very careful to emphasise throughout that "everything was done decently and in order" (1 Corinthians 14:40) during our first weekend at this Full Gospel Church in South Chard, only very briefly touching on the gift of tongues. It was obvious that some were very interested but, to our bewilderment, a few seemed resentful and even angry, and we were later accused by one or two whom we had thought of as 'pillars of the church' of being fundamentalist. If that meant believing the Bible to be the true Word of God, then that was a label we were (and are) happy to wear.

A few weeks later John and Doreen made arrangements to stay at South Chard themselves. Like us, they were baptised in water and filled with the Holy Spirit, returning home full of joy, greatly blessed. In 1969 as far as we could tell, the only other Spirit-filled Christians we knew lived quite a distance away and we were delighted that here were two friends who could share with us this new way of worship and prayer, learning together how to move in the gifts of the Spirit.

We met together in our home initially on Wednesday evenings, and were joined by two or three other friends as they, too, came into this experience. We had no intention of competing with churches so would never meet on a Sunday, but eventually met on Saturday evenings and were amazed at the folk who joined us, some travelling long distances.

How people came to know of our meetings was a mystery since it was only by word of mouth, and we were so blessed by folk who came—from Baptist, Anglican, Brethren, Quaker, Catholic backgrounds and several from the London City Mission. We never knew who would turn up on a Saturday evening, many of whom we had never met before. At times there could be 20 or more of us squeezed into our sitting room, all learning how to pray, worship and move in the gifts of the Holy Spirit.

One Saturday evening Doreen shared her concern for a neighbour who had gone into hospital and who had a dreadful fear of not only dying but also being buried alive. As we began to wait on the Lord He gave me a vivid picture of an ear, of all things. I felt stupid as I shared this but Doreen immediately told us this lady was very deaf, and so Norman led us in praying that this dear soul would somehow come to know Jesus despite her difficulties.

The following Monday Doreen met a friend who had just returned from visiting the hospital, very excited. Apparently her deaf neighbour had had a vision of Jesus on Saturday evening when He told her she was going to be with Him in heaven very soon. This had had a profound effect on her, and she had called all her family and told them what had happened. She had lost her fear completely, and wanted to put all her affairs in order!

Still in hospital, she passed away very peacefully the following Thursday, having shared with many people the wonderful miracle that had happened to her. We were all so thrilled with what the Lord had done, and how He had shown us all how to pray.

It was during a visit to Chard when Norman and I were staying in Neil and Fiona's bungalow after their wedding that we heard our eight year-old son Simon playing chords on their piano. Although he had lessons when he was six he just didn't seem to want to practice and his wise teacher advised us not to nag him, just wait a while and we'd probably find he would be keen to pick it up again in a year or two. As we listened we were amazed that all the chords he was playing were in harmony.

After a while, thinking wistfully how lovely it would be if he could eventually play for the meetings in our home in North London, we asked him if he would like us to pray with him, that the Lord would use his gift of music. He readily agreed and we simply laid hands on him and prayed that the Lord would use Simon for His glory.

We had very limited vision in those days, and we couldn't have imagined that by the time he was twelve he would be playing the organ for services in the Church. God also gave him a wonderful ability to play by ear, especially for worship, at Christian conferences in Sweden, Israel and the United States as well as here in the UK. He is a stockbroker in the City of London but continues to visit the US, leading and teaching songwriting workshops in Nashville and St Louis. His children too, are following in his musical footsteps on the flute, piano and trombone.

We so regretted that we hadn't encouraged Duncan to play the drums (which he did with great skill) but, living in suburban Oakwood, we thought it might disturb our neighbours (in hindsight, though, we should have encouraged him for all we were worth). He now encourages his own sons Keith and Luke in their music and art. Keith works in advertising and produces music for Jayzee and Timbaland, while Luke plays his guitar in London Blues clubs. Younger brother Timothy's skills are in maths and IT.

Andrew, too, played the tenor sax extremely well and sensitively, and as soon as he saw a piece of sheet music could play on sight, which apparently is very unusual. His children enjoy playing the piano, trumpet and clarinet.

As time went on Norman knew the Lord was telling him it was time for us to leave the Methodist Church. He wasn't inclined to act rashly, and we discussed how we should do it—perhaps write a letter or (my cowardly idea!) just gradually stop attending. However, the Lord had other plans and eventually impressed upon us both that we should write our letters of resignation, which we did, much to the bewilderment of many people at the Church, not least our Minister.

It must have been very hard to understand that we weren't joining another church but simply meeting with other Christians who felt as we did, knowing the Lord was leading us in a different direction. We tried so hard not to cause offence to anyone, but many thought we were being disloyal to the Methodist Church. It was very difficult to explain that we knew we had to be obedient to Jesus, not just a denomination.

Later that summer we had arranged to visit South Chard for the second time, and arranged to go camping in a field near the Manor House. It was a busy time of preparation, and the night before we were due to set off I had just bathed five year-old Andrew and was drying his hair in his bedroom using our hand-held dryer.

It must have had a serious fault and before I realised what was happening, a fierce jet of flame shot through the handle into the palm of my hand. As I dropped the dryer it burned a hole in the carpet before I had time even to turn off the switch, and I was trembling with shock when Norman, hearing a shriek, raced upstairs to see what had happened.

My first thoughts were of huge relief that the flame hadn't burnt Andrew's hair or face, and then I was conscious of intense pain. There was a hole in my palm the size of a fivepenny piece; the flame had seared through all the layers of skin and the visible flesh was red and raw. My next thoughts were of frustration and disappointment; we were planning to travel on from Chard to Polzeath in Cornwall where we loved to surf and spend long family days on the beach, and I knew it would be difficult for me to do that with such a large open sore.

Norman prayed for my healing as he gently covered the wound with a bandage, and comforted me with a cup of tea. Then we tucked Andrew into bed and resumed packing.

It was such a busy time that I completely forgot the hair dryer incident until about midnight when at last we had finished all the preparations; finally packing away the tent, cooker, pots, pans and other paraphernalia into our trailer. By then very weary, I suddenly became aware that I had had no pain since Norman had prayed for me, so I gently lifted the bandage away and peeped underneath.

Experiencing The Impossible . . .

To my utter astonishment there was no sign of a wound—just a faint shadow where it had been—*not* a blister, but a thick skin which had grown right across! Taking the bandage off I could hardly believe my eyes, and neither could Norman! You can imagine our gratitude and relief as we praised and thanked the Lord for His wonderful healing power. I could now enjoy the beach with the rest of the family—although in fact once we arrived in Chard all the boys were so enjoying life there they begged us to stay—they were having such a great time they actually preferred to be there rather than on a Cornish beach! And neither Norman nor I needed any persuasion!

We set off early and arrived at our camping site—this time in a field belonging to a friend from Chard. Thankfully we'd practised putting up our huge two bedroom tent (initially with the tarpaulin inside-out) while on holiday in the New Forest the previous year, watched with scarcely concealed smirks by other seasoned campers—a great lesson in humility!

We also invested in a funnel to avoid freezing foot showers every time we tried to fill our tiny kettle spout from an enormous billycan—and bought a new pump for our air mattresses. The previous year Norman had to inflate all five by mouth when we discovered too late that our old foot pump had broken! And five year-old Andrew, going with his big brothers to collect water in small buckets, returned with only a tiny drop of water in his bucket but his Wellington boots filled to the brim!!

So all in all a much more peaceful start to our holiday, and we relaxed for the rest of the day.

Sunday was bright and sunny, and after the morning service we discovered that it was quite usual to have a hundred or so visitors regularly staying for lunch; this was in the large Sunday School Room attached to the Church and we all sat at long trestle tables. Auntie Mill often made delicious lamb pies accompanied by salad or hot vegetables, and the deacons cheerfully provided everyone with tea and coffee from great steaming jugs.

It was humbling to be served with such willingness, and although we were among strangers we already felt we belonged there. Later that afternoon there was a Bible study after the children's Sunday School, and the evening meeting began as usual at six thirty. This was to be the pattern of our Sundays when we visited South Chard, and after several visits our new friends began to ask when we were going to move to Somerset.

We all loved being there and my darling husband was ready to make a move as soon as possible, but I was very reluctant to move away from London because my Mother had been widowed just over a year earlier and I couldn't bear to think of leaving her. Although she was very close to her sister Eileen, who lived in an adjoining flat, my only sister Jill lived in Australia so I knew how deeply my mother and auntie Eileen would miss us all. I already felt guilty at the thought of leaving them and living so far away. Added to this I knew I was at a great disadvantage: I knew our friends at South Chard had more faith to believe we *would* move there than I had faith to believe we wouldn't!

We had been told of couples who moved to Chard without jobs believing God would provide, but to my relief Norman felt very strongly that the Lord would provide a job *first* if He wanted us in the West Country. Norman was at that time a Careers Officer (known then as a Youth Employment Officer) but knew he would almost inevitably have to make a career change to obtain work in the West Country.

One of the jobs he applied for was as a Social Worker with the Church of England Children's Society (now The Children's Society) overseeing adoptions and fostering, visiting prospective parents over a period of time and then checking that all was well when the baby or child was placed with a family.

He was overjoyed when he was invited to an interview but I was on pins, still very reluctant to move away. By then I had for many nights lain awake wondering how I could ever break the news to my dear Mum and Eileen. On the day he returned from the interview his face was literally glowing, and when I asked him tentatively how it had gone, fearing the worst—that he had been offered the job—he asked what I thought the very best result would be.

"You haven't got it?" I asked hopefully.

"No", he grinned. "Better than that. They'll let me know in a few weeks' time!"

However, as the weeks went by he became more and more disappointed. He eventually telephoned the Society enquiring whether they had appointed anyone yet, and they were very apologetic that their office hadn't notified him, but yes, they had found someone else who was suitable.

Norman, never one to give up easily, decided to write and offer his services should the other applicant be unable to take up the post. In the meantime he was scouring newspapers looking for anything suitable, including bookshop management or other office work.

By then, although genuinely disappointed for him, I felt sure that there was still plenty of time if this was the right move and suggested over our morning tea in bed a few weeks later that if the Lord wanted us in South Chard, He would provide a job on a plate. Norman wouldn't have to strive for one.

About half an hour later a letter arrived in the post. It was from the Children's Society offering him the same job—but at an increased salary—the original salary having been considerably less than he was paid in London. It seemed the previous applicant couldn't afford to move away from home and had to forfeit the job after all. Norman was overjoyed, of course, and I was so glad for him but at the same time my heart sank. How was I going to break the news that we would be moving so far away? On the day I eventually had to announce the news, it needed all my courage.

To our astonishment and relief, however, Mum and Eileen took the news very stoically and without a great deal of surprise, saying they realised how much we loved visiting Chard and already had an idea it would only be a matter of time before we moved.

Although they obviously felt very sad and knew it would be hard to see us go, they gave us their blessing and said they looked forward to being able to visit us there. The Lord had truly gone before us and prepared the way! God was, even then, preparing our home and a very different way of life for us all—and although we had no inkling of it at the time, He had an even greater blessing in store for my Mum.

By now John and Doreen knew of our plans to move away and were happy to hold future meetings in their home a short distance away in Southgate, and although we were very sad in so many ways to leave we knew this was in God's plan for all of us. Eventually under John and Doreen's ministry the Southgate Fellowship, as it was then called, began to attract so many people that meetings had to be held in a hall, then in a school, where it still flourishes today under the pastoral care of John and Vicki Rawding.

John and Doreen were eventually led to move to Camden Town in central London where they ministered to many University students and travelled from time to time to Communist Eastern Europe carrying Bibles and clothes for persecuted families of pastors there. They have some amazing stories to tell.

None of us could have foreseen what we would all be doing only three years from that first visit to South Chard, and how God would bless us all in different ways.

Chapter Three

A NEW LIFE BEGINS

The first step in our move away from North London was of course to find the right home. Norman's father Jack, widowed several years earlier, would be coming with us. He was a lovely man, very much a gentleman in every sense of the word, and we began searching for a large house with suitable accommodation attached.

Despite several sorties to try to find a property, in the end Norman said he had the strangest feeling we were looking for the wrong thing in the right place, and although John and Doreen had seen a house on our behalf which seemed perfect for the family, it wouldn't have been at all suitable for Norman's father.

In despair one night, since our London home was sold and we needed to find somewhere suitable very quickly, we prayed fervently for help, and my Bible fell open at random in Exodus. My eyes were immediately drawn to verse 20 in chapter 23 accentuated in bold printing: "Behold, I send an angel before thee, to keep thee in the way, and to bring thee into the place which I have prepared". As I shared this with Norman it was the first time in many weeks that we both felt great peace; God had it all in hand, everything would work out.

In fact, only two weeks later, to our great sadness, Norman's father died very suddenly. It was a deep shock, and we put all our plans on hold for several weeks. This was something we hadn't even contemplated and was a great loss to all the family. Eventually we felt perhaps it was time to look at Rosedale, if it was still on the market. This was the house that John and Doreen had thought might be just right for us. And so we travelled to the West Country yet again . . .

We knew we were being led by the Lord to open our home to those who, like us, had heard of the church at South Chard, longing to share in the praise and worship and learn more about this wonderful move of God. When we saw Rosedale we knew we had no need to search any further; it was ideal, and the sale of our Oakwood home and the purchase of Rosedale went through very smoothly. We prepared to move house in early March 1971.

By now Neil and Fiona were married and living at the other end of our lane and as soon as they knew when we were moving they offered us accommodation for the night before completion. We gratefully accepted, and after checking that all was in order for the following day we settled our little black and white cat, Sally, with her basket, saucer of milk and litter tray in the corner of the empty sitting room of our new home.

Moving day itself was very cold with a flutter of snowflakes, and when we opened the door of the sitting room we were startled to find that Sally had completely disappeared. The windows and door were closed and since there was nowhere for her to hide we were completely mystified. Then suddenly we heard a scraping noise and the poor little thing literally fell into the fireplace. Something must have frightened her in the night and she took refuge up the chimney—but thankfully buttering her paws and giving her another long drink of milk with her breakfast calmed her down, and we found a quiet spot where she could feel safe in her basket and settle happily in her new home.

Rosedale, in Snowdon Cottage Lane, Chard, was described as an old cottage, but was in fact a spacious house with six bedrooms and flint walls 23" thick, built around 1780—and when we were shown the Deeds we discovered that a Reverend Hawkins was the very first occupant all those years ago! Some of the rooms still had the original shutters, and we discovered later that under the wallpaper the kitchen walls were lined with horsehair, wattle and daub (interwoven twigs plastered with a mixture of clay and water). We were very glad of the skills of Brian, a local builder who later replastered and redecorated for us.

Mrs. Sully, the former owner and a Christian whose family had lived in and around Chard for generations, had apparently had this house on the market three times before but taken it off the market again each time. However, she later told Norman that when he stood on her doorstep as she opened the door to meet him for the first time, she *knew* Rosedale belonged to him—she actually said that—and that she was to sell the property to him.

A New Life Begins

The Angel of the Lord must certainly have kept this home for us to be used for His purposes, and from the moment we moved in we had an extraordinary sense of warmth and welcome every time we walked through the front door. It had everything we could possibly need, and inside our new home our three boys played hide and seek—there were so many nooks, crannies and cupboards it wasn't difficult to be genuinely lost! From the two large attic guest bedrooms were panoramic views towards Windwhistle Hill in the distance and we could just see the Town Hall in the centre of Chard and hear its clock chiming the hours.

Rosedale's lovely quarter of an acre garden was bordered by huge fir trees and included a greenhouse, potting shed and log store. There were many flowering shrubs, including a glorious heavily perfumed yellow broom. We stepped from the back porch on to a large area of semi-circular lawn edged with staddle stones, those mysterious stone mushrooms that were used to help stack hay many years ago. In the centre stood an ancient sundial.

Steps led to a lower lawn where several rose-covered archways framed the paths, and at the far end of the garden a large wooden summer house became the children's den where, on hot, sunny summer afternoons they could play with their friends and enjoy tall glasses of lemonade and fairy cakes for tea.

We fell in love with Rosedale, and when we moved in on a bitterly cold March day we discovered hundreds of tiny Devon violets growing at the end of the long garden where a gate led to a path to the High Street. I still have vivid memories of pinching ourselves in disbelief during those early days as we looked across the hills, listening to the glorious dawn chorus from tall cypresses as though birds were singing in a vast cathedral.

The long garden, lined with these huge trees, had obviously been lovingly cared for and occasionally we would stand on the lawn and murmur that quick prayer: "HELP!" since our lives were so busy there was very little time for serious gardening. Later we were so grateful to find a gardener, Mr. Wickens, a dear old chap who smoked like a chimney despite having only one lung, and who would regularly weed and nurture this huge plot for us.

After living most of our lives in a North London suburb it was still difficult to believe we could actually be here in Somerset and less than half an hour from Lyme Regis, a beautiful old fishing village. We especially loved visiting the beautiful sandy beach, the old smuggler's inn and quaint shops near The Cobb, the ancient sea wall.

Our nearest seaside town while living in North London as children in the 1940s was Southend, over three hours away by steam train. We would leave the house at around eight o'clock in the morning, spend the day in Southend and return home at about ten-thirty in the evening, absolutely exhausted. After all these years I still live near the sea (though now on the south Sussex coast) and never take for granted the privilege. I love all its moods, from summer's shimmering blues to winter's sometimes savage grey.

There was only one other thing that had really bothered me and kept me awake at nights—that we might either be too busy with our guests and neglect our boys or too busy with the boys and neglect our guests—it seemed a no-win situation. In fact, to our astonishment instead of the boys resenting our visitors they were always asking who was coming next—they really enjoyed meeting so many new and interesting people.

Some offered to play cricket with them or show them how to play musical instruments—and one guest was incredibly popular when he showed them how to do magic tricks. Geoffrey (I forget his surname) owned a magic shop in Watford and our boys were tickled pink when he gave them a few tricks of their own before returning home, including a smoke bomb which, put into our car's exhaust, unnerved their Dad no end!

Memorable, too, was the fork which looked perfectly normal but would bend backwards as though it was broken—unsuspecting guests were given it until at last it fell apart! One lovely couple gave us a dinghy which was a particular blessing when Father Joseph, a Catholic priest, came to stay. Our guests were very welcome and in the end I was the only one insisting on an occasional much-needed break.

We knew there was more than enough to do on that first wintry day when we moved in and were very touched when one of our friends from the church, Jenny Lamb, happened to be passing, saw the removals van and immediately offered to help us unpack. We were so grateful: by the end of that day, thanks to the extra pair of hands, all the kitchen cupboards were filled and crockery and cutlery stacked neatly away. Although most of our clothes were in black sacks (no built in wardrobes) and there would be much redecorating to do over the next months, there was no immediate hurry.

Or so we thought . . . for the very next weekend we had our first visitor—Norman's cousin Jean. She had been his babysitter and often prayed for him when she looked after him as a little boy. There were no curtains at the windows and it would take several weeks to sort us out, but it really didn't matter. It didn't take long to realize that what *did* matter was that people seeking more of Jesus were warmly welcomed, returning home (hopefully) with spiritual and emotional needs met. Jean was the first of so many people who were tremendous blessings to us.

What astonished me was the discovery that although I had never liked it, suddenly cooking didn't seem difficult at all, and over the next few years it became a normal way of life to cater for as many as twelve people. During Bank Holidays there would be even more visitors—sometimes sleepers overflowing to the floor of Norman's study and the spacious landing! It had to be by the grace of God!

Here is where I should share with you how incredible it was for me to be able to tackle catering *at all*, let alone on this scale. My young sister Jill and I were brought up during the Second World War, my Mother working desperately long hours, most days from early morning until nearly midnight because money was exceedingly short. We were very blessed to have been able to live with my grandparents; if they hadn't taken us into their home Jill and I could well have gone into care when our parents were divorced in 1942.

A New Life Begins

My Dad was away in the Air Force, so sadly we saw very little of him, and although it was desperately needed he gave my Mother little or no maintenance. Grandmother also worked all day, providing dinners, pies, scones, cakes and other essentials for the little cafe rented by my grandparents over thirty minutes' walk away (since there was no public or private transport) and evenings were mostly taken up with baking for the next day.

Food coupons were also very scarce and couldn't be frittered away on experimental cooking, so almost the first opportunity we had to learn was at school, where I soon realised I wasn't at all gifted in that direction (my margarine was always bright yellow when everyone else had managed to beat theirs white), although my sister was brilliant at making and icing cakes.

Although I had known Norman for 6 years—I was 15, he was 17 when we met—when at last we were married in 1953 it may sound unbelievable but it wasn't until we were in the taxi on the way home from our honeymoon that it suddenly hit me like a ton of bricks that I was now expected to make every meal for my new husband and myself for perhaps the next 50 years or so. In the 1950s there was no such thing as a "New Man" and cooking was nowhere on Norman's horizon!

Not only that, but dinner had to be prepared at the end of a long day (I worked full-time, too, as a secretary) after strap-hanging on the Underground at eight o'clock in the morning from North London into the West End and back again at around 6pm.

We were both exhausted when we arrived home from work. Since it took ages to light the tiny coal fire and warm our sitting room, it wasn't until bedtime that it was really comfortable—and too late—to relax in. In those days there wasn't such a thing as a launderette and we certainly couldn't afford luxuries like a washing machine, vacuum cleaner or refrigerator, so life was very full and intensely hard work. Every time we spilled water on the ancient iron-topped cooker it immediately went rusty and had to be everlastingly wiped and polished.

Apart from the enormous effort (for me!) needed to cook the most basic meals such as sausage, mash and tinned peas I had a go at making sponge cakes, but they almost always turned out like very thin frisbees stuck together with butter cream. I never discovered, either, why most of the fruit in my Christmas cakes sank like lead to the bottom—I could have filled the hollow in the middle with tinned fruit or a few flowers.

However, one evening a few weeks after we were married all my family called to see us and during the evening my mother described with enthusiasm a very quick and easy snack. She told me I could even make it the day before it was needed. "Oh good—anything to make life a bit easier!" I thought. So I grabbed a pen and paper and took down the recipe. My downfall was having one ear on everyone else's conversation and thereby missing a vital ingredient, but I didn't know that at the time and was determined to try this macaroni cheese dish the next day.

When we shopped for the macaroni we were surprised that the recipe apparently needed a whole pound, which looked quite a lot. I knew nothing whatsoever about pasta and assumed it must shrink in the cooking. I emptied the packet into my smallest saucepan full of boiling water and turned to collect the rest of the ingredients—flour, cheese, margarine, salt and pepper.

When I turned back I was very surprised to see the macaroni at the top of the pan already, so poured it quickly into a larger one, but by the time I found the grater it was boiling over. By now gritting my teeth (so much needless washing-up) I poured it into the last and biggest saucepan we had and watched like a hawk until it came right to the top once more.

By now it was so heavy it took both hands and all my strength to strain the pan through the colander into the sink, and even my inexperienced eyes could see there was enough macaroni to feed us for a week.

Then came the interesting bit—my very first attempt at making cheese sauce. I measured margarine, flour and grated cheese into a little pan and shook the salt and pepper over it, waiting with interest for it to melt into a lovely smooth sauce.

However, as I watched, an astonishing thing happened. It turned almost immediately into solid toffee, riveted to the sides of the pan. I was horrified. It was the last bit of cheese in the house and the cupboard was bare. Nothing for it, in desperation I grabbed the largest screwdriver Norman could find and chiselled the toffee off the sides of the pan.

It would only come off in little nuggets, and the fairest way I could think of was to divide them between us, explaining in response to Norman's bewilderment that they were cheese sauce. I was of course told later that I'd omitted that vital ingredient—milk—as I wrote the recipe—which should have included only a *quarter* of a pound of macaroni.

As I presented Norman with this massive plateful of pasta he didn't say a lot (he had learned already that it wasn't wise to criticise my efforts at the end of a long day) but we struggled doggedly through about half our portions, occasionally finding the odd cheese nugget with cries of pleasure (and spending the next five minutes trying to extract them from our teeth).

That wasn't all. The only thing I could find for dessert was one small dish of stewed apple and, since we were always starving by the time we got home from work, I tried to work out how I could multiply this for both of us. Then I had a sudden brainwave. Of *course!* We had plenty of macaroni left—enough to feed at least another family—I'd simply add it to the apple! (Unfortunately, though, forgetting it needed sugar). I was so relieved to throw the remainder in the bin.

After this fiasco all my long-suffering saint of a husband said very gently was: "Actually Molly, I should have mentioned this before, but I've never really *liked* macaroni!" This happened over 50 years ago, and I've never dared to make it since.

A real turning point came when I was given a Sunbeam Mixer. At last, after 15 years my efforts actually began (almost) to resemble pictures in recipe books! Cooking will never be my passion, though, and even now the thought of spending a whole evening with a wooden spoon whipping up something edible still fills me with dread, but you can begin to understand what a miracle the Lord had to do before I could even begin to cater for so many people.

Later, when we were led by God to open a 10 bedroom <u>hotel</u>—with no catering experience apart from our years at Rosedale—people were actually coming back every year for *"the lovely food!"* they told us. Only He can take us right through the impossible to prove that although we know *we* haven't the ability, with Him <u>all</u> things are possible!

Chapter Four
EVERY DAY SOMETHING NEW . . .

As time went by we realised what a privilege it was to have fellowship with so many (mostly!) lovely Christians. Although Norman had taken this job with the Children's Society at just over half his London wage and we would never dream of charging our guests, the Lord always provided enough to abundantly cover our costs.

From that first weekend we had literally hundreds of people to stay, sometimes at weekends, sometimes midweek. It could be very tiring, of course, and after a while we invested in a dishwasher and hired Valerie, a cheerful, apple-cheeked local lady who helped out one morning a week. There were always beds to change, cleaning to be done, and with so many visitors and three growing boys plenty of washing and ironing, but mostly they were very happy and fulfilling days, and during our years at Rosedale the Lord did some wonderful miracles.

Every Day Something New...

For instance at Whitsun weekend a couple of months after our move to Chard, we had a full complement of guests and twelve of us for dinner at midday. All morning they and other visitors had popped in and out of the kitchen while I was trying to prepare the meal, a simple shepherd's pie with apple crumble to follow. The Church had their Conference at the Guildhall in the centre of Chard which began at 2.30 pm, so we planned lunch for one o'clock sharp.

However, as soon as the meal was ready to serve I suddenly realised I had completely forgotten to cook at least 3lbs of cabbage now staring at me from the vegetable rack. I was horrified—after more than twenty years of cooking I knew there would be only enough food to fill small tea plates, and I had no time to prepare and cook the cabbage before we all needed to leave for the Conference.

"Lord, you know I didn't deliberately forget!" I prayed in desperation. "Please help me, You've somehow got to multiply this for us or we shall all be starving by the middle of the afternoon!"

In those days we had no freezer—or even a refrigerator—and I searched through the store cupboard but all I could find was one medium tin of peas. Just about enough for four helpings. Ah, well.

I sighed, put the peas into a pan to heat and began to serve the shepherd's pie, a tablespoonful on each of the twelve plates. To my astonishment there was still two-thirds left, so I served another twelve helpings—and this was incredible—there was still about a third left in this ordinary baking tin!

Then I began to serve the peas, and the same thing happened. There was a good heaped tablespoonful of peas for everyone! And by the time I had finished, each plate was piled high with ample shepherd's pie and vegetables. By now I was inwardly praising the Lord with all my heart—but didn't say anything to anyone until towards the end of the meal when I asked Dennis, one of our guests who was profoundly deaf, if he would like some apple crumble. Astonishingly, he was more than satisfied, gesturing that he was very full and had absolutely no room for dessert!

It was only then that I shared the wonder of what the Lord Jesus had done for us, and we gave Him all the glory. This kind of miracle was something that happened a number of times just when it was needed most.

One sunny afternoon at teatime a couple of years later we had a similar situation. As usual we had folk who dropped in to see us before the evening meeting and again as usual we invited them to stay for tea. It wasn't until it was time to set the table I suddenly realised that for the very first time I hadn't a piece of cake or even a biscuit anywhere in the house. Absolutely nothing. By now I was praying very hard that large plates of bread and butter with pots of Marmite and jam would somehow be enough to satisfy everyone. Then I spread them out on the table, together with the cups and saucers normally set out on the sideboard—trying to make it look less empty!

Just as I had made the tea and called everyone in to the dining room the front doorbell rang. When I opened the door Rosemary, the wife of Ian Andrews, one of the ministers from the Church, was standing on the step holding a huge iced chocolate cake on a plate—even with a pretty doily!—ready to place on the table!

"How did you know?" I asked in amazement.

"Know what?" she replied. "I was baking with Fiona (the same Fiona who had introduced us to Chard) at her bungalow" (just at the other end of the lane) "and when mine was finished the Lord suddenly told me very clearly to bring it along to you!"

I gave her a big hug, invited her to stay and thanked her profusely, explaining why it was so needed and what perfect timing—and I was so grateful for her obedience. The importance of learning to listen and obey God's voice as she had done was a real lesson to us, and such a blessing.

I took the cake into the dining room and placed it in the centre of the table, sharing with everyone what a wonderful thing our Lord had done—and what wonderful timing! He had proved Himself once again to be Jehovah Jireh indeed—our Divine Provider! I marvelled that He would care about such a small thing that meant so much to us.

A few months after moving in we realised something had to be done about the kitchen. With so many visitors coming and going it was spacious but very inadequate, and we desperately needed workspace with plenty of cupboards and drawers. We were recommended a local builder, Brian, and when he came to investigate he discovered that the walls would need replastering and he had to insulate the lower part against damp, since there was no damp course.

He was a quick and thorough worker, and all the painting, plastering and plumbing was completed in good time.

It was almost teatime on a warm September afternoon when he was putting finishing touches to the kitchen. Bright and welcoming, paintwork and cupboards were now sparkling white with bright yellow sunflowers running riot over white walls. All that remained to be done was the glueing of the last pine worktop, and the highly inflammable adhesive Brian was using had such a pungent smell that we had to open the windows wide. It was thrilling to see the complete transformation that was taking place, but I was glad to disappear into the sitting room to finish the ironing.

A few days earlier we had been saying our farewells to visitors when the telephone rang. Norman took the call. It was from a friend who had had a particular word of Scripture for us impressed upon her from Psalm 4, verse 8: "I will both lay me down in peace and sleep; for thou, Lord, only makest me dwell in safety".

It seemed a strange verse to give us—after all, what could possibly happen to a house as solid as this that had lasted for over two centuries without mishap? I was too busy to be occupied with it for long, but was to be reminded of it again on this lovely autumn day.

As I stood folding the newly-ironed shirts, watching sunlight dappling through the trees and wondering how Norman's business trip was going, my thoughts were suddenly shattered by a frantic yell from the kitchen.

"Molly, come quickly! *Quickly!* Galvanised into action, I shot through the hall, my heart suddenly pounding as I saw with horror a cloud of thick black smoke pouring from the open kitchen door. As I reached it I could hear a loud roar as huge flames leapt from the glued work surfaces almost to the ceiling, which was covered in newly painted polystyrene tiles. Fumes from the glue had been ignited by the tiny pilot light in a new gas refrigerator that I had forgotten to switch off.

By this time Brian was leaping frantically backwards and forwards trying to beat out the fire with a towel, and I involuntarily did the first thing that sprang to mind—took a deep breath and blew hard at the inferno with all my might!! Just for a second Brian looked at me in total disbelief, and the next moment flung a bucket of water over the blaze. This time I grabbed a bucket and did likewise. It was very frightening for a few minutes as we rushed breathlessly to and fro, and the acrid smell of burning glue made us cough as it filled the kitchen.

At last, however, the flames were extinguished and we stood helplessly with hearts pounding wildly, watching millions of greasy flecks like black snowflakes drift down from the ceiling, smothering us in a thick fog. Although Brian was standing only a few feet away I had to peer shortsightedly through the inky gloom to see his blackened face. He was staring bleakly at the burnt worktop, pitch black now where the glue had caught fire, obviously pondering all his seemingly wasted effort.

As the flecks gradually settled we could see to our dismay that the entire kitchen was covered from floor to ceiling in a grey, greasy film. When I opened the cupboards I groaned inwardly as I saw cups, plates, utensils and even food, covered in dark specks. Knowing Norman wouldn't be returning until the following evening and feeling very tired already, my heart sank at the thought of the hours of work ahead.

"I quite thought he'd gone up then", said Brian in his soft Somerset accent. His expression was a curious mixture of dejection and relief. "In fact, I was just about to call the Fire Brigade in case the ceiling caught".

He was looking sideways at me now; the whole kitchen looked so desolate I knew he was wondering how I would react—become hysterical, perhaps, or burst into tears. But as I looked at the ceiling, now a dirty grey but miraculously intact, I breathed a silent prayer of thankfulness to my Heavenly Father that the fire hadn't spread to the bathroom above.

As I did so, to my utter astonishment I felt a great surge of joy welling up inside. What did Jesus say, something about "Out of your belly shall flow rivers of living water!" (John 7:38) Suddenly I wanted to laugh—but I daren't; I was trying hard without much success not to grin, the corners of my mouth twitching, and glancing at Brian I knew he was already imagining the worst—the shock had sent me quietly mad!

Instead, "Oh well, never mind", I said consolingly. "It's a bit like giving your brand new car a good kick on its first day, then if it gets a knock later it's not quite such a disaster, but

Brian, I'm so sorry all your hard work has been spoiled, and it was all my fault!"

He looked immensely relieved, and said he would begin by mopping up the water, which by now had made black puddles everywhere. I was still inwardly reeling from my own reaction, which I knew could only have been the Lord's doing. Suddenly that verse from Psalm 4 flashed into my mind; *of course!* It was Father's assurance and provision for this very time.

Later I grabbed my Bible and read the end of the Psalm, filled with deep gratitude once more at the words of verse 7: "You have given me greater joy than those who have abundant harvests of grain and wine"*(NIV)*. I hadn't read that verse before, and could only marvel at God's goodness in giving such reassurance beforehand.

By now it was almost teatime and I expected the children home at any moment. I made preparations for the marathon mopping-up operation and when Brian had left and tea was over I broke the news to the boys that the entire kitchen would need cleaning immediately and I needed their help. They grumbled for a moment or two then, unexpectedly, quite cheerfully grabbed the tea towels and washed and dried the contents of all the cupboards for me while I scrubbed the woodwork and sunflower covered vinyl walls.

Astonishingly, by 8.30 we had finished, and except for the blackened work surfaces and grey ceiling which now needed repainting, it was almost difficult to believe that there had been such a dangerous fire in the kitchen at all. God had, in fact, blessed a situation which could have ended tragically—if the fire *had* spread to the bathroom it would have been very difficult to contain without a huge amount of damage.

And it was a delight to work in when it was completed at last!

At about this time his best friend, Philip, invited Duncan to stay at his home in North London for a few days. Before our move to Somerset he lived opposite us with his family in Oakwood. I couldn't see any reason why Duncan shouldn't, but Norman felt very strongly that Philip should come to stay with us *first*.

Philip duly arrived one Saturday morning a few weeks later, and after exploring the area with Duncan he began asking questions about Chard and the reasons why we had moved there. When he learned that Norman and I were going to the church that evening he immediately asked if he could come too. We were delighted; we felt never to pressure folk to come—it had to be voluntary! So we *all* trooped off, having no inkling of the effect it would have on young Philip.

The ministry that evening was centred on water baptism, and partway through the evening Philip began to tremble until he was eventually shaking quite violently. He was obviously being deeply affected by the Holy Spirit, and at the end of that meeting he asked if he could be baptised the next morning.

We asked one of the elders, and he and several others took Philip aside and explained through the Scriptures the significance of water baptism—being buried with Jesus Christ and rising with Him in newness of life. Philip was adamant that this was what God was showing him, and so the next morning, to the delight of us all, he was baptised, radiant when he emerged from the water.

When we returned home for lunch, to our amazement he brought down from his room his "Little Book of Mao's Sayings" (apparently he had become a fervent communist during his time at senior school), all his drugs and syringe, and showed us the needle marks in his arms.

He told us that he had been to parties where drugs were thrown into a bowl on the table and he and his friends would sample them; at one stage, horrifyingly he had tried to fly out of an upstairs window. He burnt Mao's book and asked us to dispose of the drugs and syringe. He assured us that he wouldn't need these ever again, and we learned later that on his return to school he was converting all his friends to Christianity!

We were so grateful that the Lord had shown Norman that he should stay with us first—it could have been difficult for Duncan not to have been drawn into the drugs scene if he had initially gone to stay with Philip. They kept in touch for several years, until we heard the sad news that Philip had died in a car accident in his early twenties. Thank God he knew his Saviour.

As time went on many folk came to stay, friends and those we had never met before. One of these was a Catholic priest from Germany called Father Joseph. One of our friends who was also a minister at the Church, Andrew Jordan, had known him for some while and explained that Joseph longed so much for a real experience of God that he had delved into all kinds of religions, including Sikhism, Buddhism and Islam—each one with his whole heart and being—but never found what he was searching for.

When he heard about the Church at South Chard it must have seemed a real answer to prayer, and Norman arranged to meet him at Taunton Station; both wearing pocket handkerchiefs to identify one another. Joseph was so anxious not to be missed that his handkerchief flowed almost to his waist!

We were a little apprehensive, wondering if he would be exceedingly "religious"—but we need not have worried. He was a gentle, humble man in his forties who just wanted to find his Heavenly Father.

During the following Sunday morning service, he stood next to us while praise and worship was at its highest. Suddenly he gave a great roar and fell under the power of the Holy Spirit, being wonderfully delivered from all the demonic religious spirits as he lay on the floor. The deacons (there were as yet no elders) gathered around and prayed for him, and as the depth of worship increased even more, we praised the Lord with all of our hearts for what He was doing.

In just a short while Joseph was set completely free! It was such amazing proof that God truly does inhabit the praises of His people!

That evening he was baptised in water—apparently the only person who had ever leapt right out of the Church's deep baptistry afterwards instead of walking up the steps, he was so elated, and shortly afterwards filled with the Holy Spirit!

His search over at last, he would often walk around our garden early in the morning deep in the study of his Bible and share with us over breakfast what the Lord Jesus was showing him. Andrew had told us that Joseph had a brilliant mind and was a teacher of novitiates at Bonn University before they entered into priesthood.

While he was with us we asked if he would like a day on the beach. He beamed with delight! He was born in Bavaria, had never been anywhere near the coast and always dreamed of going to the seaside! So we and the children took him to Sandy Bay in Exmouth, where he changed into his black (of course!) swimming trunks behind a large waste bin and spent the next hour or two in the sea where we all had great fun trying (but not succeeding!) to sit in our little dinghy without falling off.

Later while we were drying in the warmth of the sun on the beach a little boy came up to him and offered a lick of his ice cream, while a tiny girl wanted to put sun lotion on his arms. He was entranced, and said it was one of the happiest days of his life. We reflected on the wonder that God can meet the deepest needs and satisfy everyone's hunger for Himself in so many different ways.

Before Joseph returned home we asked gently how he would equate his transforming experiences with the worship of Mary in the Roman Catholic Church. He replied that he had asked the Lord about this, and felt very strongly that when he returned to Germany he should share with his pupils and fellow priests all he now knew about Jesus, being born again and filled with the Holy Spirit. It was sad to see him go; he was such a genuinely humble man, and we felt truly privileged to have shared with him such a life-changing experience.

Not long after this Father Radici came to stay. He was a Russian Orthodox priest who told us that he longed so much to know God and the reality of Jesus there were times when he would flagellate himself with whips and kneel for literally hours on a stone floor wearing sackcloth. He spent much of his time at his monastery painting icons to sell, and with the other monks lived very frugally, mostly on vegetables from their garden. He looked very like a grey-bearded Father Christmas!

Before he left Father Radici thought it would be interesting to try Marmite on his bread for the first time, and although we urged him to spread only a *tiny* portion on his buttered slice he was quite generous with it. Watching his expression we assured him he honestly didn't *have* to eat it if it was that horrible, but he struggled gamely until the last mouthful! "Never again!" he shuddered, but laughed heartily at himself along with the rest of us.

Like Father Joseph, Radici was baptised in water and filled with the Holy Spirit before returning home, determined to share his experience with others longing for the reality of a Heavenly Father and Saviour. As he prepared to leave us we told him how impressed we were with his gentleness and the very real humility we had seen in him. "Ah yes," he replied with a sigh and a twinkle in his eye, "I am very proud of my humility!"

Many of the folk who came to stay needed prayer and counselling. One couple who arrived with their 3 year-old had marriage problems, but despite trying not to, as they came through our front door I couldn't help recoiling when I saw Garry, their little son. His face was ashen and he was so fair he seemed to have no eyebrows or lashes. Added to that his nose was constantly running with thick catarrh.

By the time we went to bed I hadn't once felt able to go within arm's reach, let alone give him a cuddle, and I knew I needed to ask the Lord's help to really love this little boy. After all, how could we minister to the parents if we rejected their little son? I prayed fervently for help.

The next morning while I was preparing breakfast Garry came running into the kitchen with a beaming smile, nose still oozing thick catarrh. Without thinking I immediately bent down and took him in my arms, feeling a great surge of love. It wasn't until we went into breakfast that I suddenly realised what the Lord had done and how faithfully He had answered prayer. Such a seemingly small thing, but once again something I knew just wasn't possible without His help.

Chapter Five

IN EVERYTHING GIVE THANKS!

During those early days after moving into Rosedale, there was an occasional sharp cracking sound right along the main staircase wall. We assumed it was simply because the house was so old the walls were reacting to changes in temperature, but when it happened later than usual one evening it was so loud it startled all of us and awoke six year-old Andrew, who began screaming in terror. It was very unusual for him to react in this way, and we began to realise there could be more to this than met the eye.

After we comforted him and he had fallen asleep again we laid hands on the wall and in the Name of Jesus bound the demonic power behind the noise and consequent fear and commanded that the noise should stop forthwith and never ever happen again. The Scripture tells us God has given all believers authority over *all* the power of Satan (Luke 9:1) and we learned to pray this kind of prayer many times over the years. Thankfully we never ever heard that noise again.

We were learning, in the atmosphere of real faith in miracles and blessing, to rely more and more on the Lord, and one night Andrew called out "Mummy, mummy, come quickly, I've got a nose-bleed!"

I stumbled out of bed half asleep, but was shocked to see so much blood all over the pillowcase and sheet and it was really pumping out of his nose. I rushed to the bathroom to bring a damp flannel to wipe his face.

"Can you try and pinch your nose to stop the bleeding?" I asked. But it made him choke. Now I'm not good with blood, and suddenly the room began to spin. I knew I'd faint if I couldn't lie flat, so in desperation I laid hands on him and literally gasped "In the Name of Jesus be made whole!" before staggering back into our bedroom, throwing myself on the bed.

"Norman, quick, wake up! Andrew's got a dreadful nosebleed and I feel so faint I can't do anything for him. Please go and see if he's all right!"

A few moments later Norman was back in bed again.

"I don't know what all the fuss was about. His nose isn't bleeding now and he's nearly asleep!" I think he thought I might have got him out of bed under false pretences, and when I took a peek at Andrew a little later it was quite true; the bleeding had stopped and he was by then already fast asleep. In the morning when we saw the heavy bloodstains on his pillow and bedding which weren't so apparent in the dark the night before, we knew God had wonderfully and immediately answered prayer.

On another occasion Simon was on his way home from school when, indulging in a bit of horseplay, another lad punched him so hard in the chest that he had difficulty in breathing and was unusually pale. We were extremely concerned that perhaps a rib was broken or his lung punctured but although we prayed for him nothing changed.

By then we were wondering if Ian Andrews (Rosemary's husband) who lived nearby and has a powerful healing ministry, was available and telephoned him straight away. There was no reply and he could well have been away travelling, so we decided it would be wise to make an appointment to have Simon examined by our doctor—but before we had time to do that Ian suddenly appeared on the doorstep, having no idea we had tried to contact him.

We were so grateful, and after a brief prayer the colour came back into Simon's cheeks, he began to breathe normally and immediately went out to play football as though nothing had happened. What a wonderful Heavenly Father we have!

During the first couple of years at Rosedale my Mother and her sister Eileen came to stay—very happy times—but we had prayed for my Mum's salvation for over twenty years and longed for her to know the Lord as her Saviour.

Then one day it was as if my eyes were opened as I saw the verses in John 14: 13-14: "And whatsoever you shall ask in My name, that will I do, that the Father may be glorified in the Son. If ye shall ask *anything* in My name, I will do it". I suddenly realised that this was a promise for *her*. So I talked to the Lord and told Him I knew He had heard my prayers and so I would never ask again for her salvation, but would just praise and thank Him for doing it.

Well, the next eighteen months weren't too comfortable—the enemy tried so hard to cause dissent—but whenever everything seemed to be going pear-shaped as far as she was concerned I resolved never to say anything but "Thank You, Lord, for saving my darling Mum!"

A few weeks later my sister Jill and her husband were returning to Australia after their time in England, my Mother having been so upset when they first moved there that she had had a breakdown. We arrived at my Mother's London flat where my sister and her family were waiting for their taxi to the airport. As we walked up the long flight of stairs all I could think of, apart from having to say our sad farewells to Jill and Peter and the children, was Mum's state of mind.

However, as we walked into the big kitchen where they were all gathered and Mum was sitting at the table, talking to them very calmly and quite happily, the Lord spoke to me very clearly in an almost audible voice: "She is born again and belongs to Me now!"

I was astonished and thrilled, and over the years often wondered how she was saved, but we only know she had a very real relationship with her Saviour. Often after that day when I telephoned and she asked how things were and perhaps I was troubled about something, she would simply say, "Now, Molly, you know the Lord is looking after everything, don't you?" She could never have said that, or had such quiet confidence, before.

This was confirmed in a wonderful way a couple of years later. She had been diagnosed with Parkinson's Disease and pernicious anaemia, both incurable, and when we visited her in St Anne's Hospital in London, to our consternation she was in a small side ward with a woman who was obviously dying—and Mum looked deathly ill herself.

After our visit we returned to Eileen's flat and we told her how sad we were that my mother had had such an unhappy life (divorced from my Dad whom she dearly loved and always struggling with finances, so lonely she had turned to alcohol and even tried to commit suicide). I remarked that it was almost as though she had been cursed.

At this Eileen looked startled. "Well, you know she *was* cursed, don't you?"

"No—who by, a gypsy?"

"It was your great aunt Ivy. She was a very jealous and bitter woman who cursed your Mother when she was only 17 years old—such a horrible curse I couldn't even repeat it."

At last—this explained a great deal, and as soon as we returned to Somerset that evening we prayed and asked God to lift the power of the curse. We thanked Him for the precious Sword of the Spirit (the Word of God) and with it severed her from every effect of the curse and asked that the blood of Jesus cleanse her. Then we bound the power of Satan in Jesus' Name; loosed to my mother the healing power of Jesus Christ and gave Him thanks and praise.

When we visited her in hospital again just a week later she had been moved to a large, happy ward and looked so well and contented, we were thrilled. Then the nurse came to give her tablets, but to my consternation she wasn't given her blue Parkinson 'torpedoes'. When she had forgotten to take them the previous summer it had caused seizures, and on one awful occasion when her doctor had been called, her heart actually stopped and had to be massaged back to life.

So I quietly excused myself and had a word with the nurse, asking if she shouldn't have had her Parkinson pill. She looked a little embarrassed and said she couldn't understand how Mr. H. the consultant could have made such a mistake (her illness had also been confirmed by four other doctors and consultants in London and Somerset!) but my Mother didn't *have* Parkinson's.

"What about her pernicious anaemia then?" I asked.

"No, there's no sign of that either!" said the nurse. My mother had had injections twice a week for the previous two years and was told she would have to continue with them for the rest of her life!

When I asked what the new tablets were for, she explained that they had found a lack of vitamins in her bone marrow, so these were just 'topping her up'!

So I returned to the ward. "Mum!" I said. "Do you know you don't have Parkinson's any more—or pernicious anaemia. The Lord has healed you!"

She didn't look at all surprised. "I knew something must have happened", she said with a gentle smile. "Look at my hands!" When she held them out to me it was the first time I could ever remember that they weren't trembling. The relief and gratitude we all felt was overwhelming.

That was by no means all. When she arrived home from hospital, having had an alcohol problem for many years, the first thing Eileen did was to offer her a glass of sherry. We were horrified, knowing she hadn't needed a drink for over sixteen weeks, but it was impossible at that moment to comment. Even more so when Eileen offered her *another*—but to our astonishment and huge relief, she simply said, "No thanks dear, that was very nice!"

And from then on she could have an occasional sherry without needing more—which for many years had been an impossibility! It was only then that we realised with great gratitude that the Lord had done yet another wonderful miracle in her life.

The following year she went on her very first overseas holiday—with Eileen—to visit my sister in Australia!

Although life at Rosedale was very happy, there were inevitably some times of testing, especially when we were overtired. During one of these the Lord had to teach us how to say "No" when we were asked to do something we just weren't meant to be doing, yet felt guilty if we couldn't comply. We had for a while felt very puzzled because some guests would come for a week and we'd feel quite fresh at the end of their stay—others would come for a short weekend and it would take at least a week to recover!

As we prayed about this, the Lord reminded us again that "out of our belly flow rivers of living water" (John 7:38). If we were asked, for instance, to have someone to stay but felt reluctant and very uneasy inside, He showed us it wasn't because we were being lazy but because He was trying to speak to us and there were times we needed to refuse. At the same time, even if when asked we felt exhausted, we knew if we felt real peace within that it was OK to agree.

Even then it wasn't easy to say no, until the Lord showed us that it wasn't only for *our* sakes that we might have to refuse, but we weren't always the right people He had in mind for our visitors. This really put our minds at rest and made it so much easier to make the right choice.

One evening a few years after moving to Rosedale I went into Andrew's bedroom to say goodnight when he suddenly burst into tears (*very* unlike him) exclaiming "I hate him, I hate him, I'll kill him if he doesn't stop!"

Very perturbed, I asked him who he was talking about and what he had done. It turned out that an older boy at his grammar school waited for him at every break and lunchtime, pushed him out of the queue and kicked him. This was at the beginning of the new term—unknown to us he had been doing it for most of last term and Andrew had hoped this would be a fresh start, but unfortunately the bullying simply continued.

"Why didn't you tell us this before?" I said. "We must go and see the Headmaster straight away!"

"No, no, you can't, Mum!" he cried. "It's the headmaster's son Roger who's doing it!"

I was nonplussed for a few moments, praying silently to know what on earth I could do that wouldn't make the situation worse. We could hardly go up to the Head and tell him his little darling was kicking the living daylights out of our son. Then the Lord said very simply: "Pray . . ." and reminded me of a well-known Bible story.

"Andrew, do you remember what happened with David and Goliath?" He visibly brightened. "Do you mean I should take a catapult to school?" I laughed despite myself. "No, I certainly don't! But do you remember how God helped David kill that huge Goliath with only one stone? Now, do you believe that if we pray together God can do something about this bullying?"

Andrew is very honest, and hesitated for a few moments before replying.

"Yes, I do."

"Right then, we're going to ask the Lord what's making this boy behave like this and pray about it." As we prayed, the Lord showed me to take Scriptural authority over Roger and bind every spirit of resentment, insecurity, inferiority, spitefulness and bullying. (Matthew 18:18—"Verily I say unto you, whatsoever ye shall bind on earth shall be bound in heaven: and whatsoever ye shall loose on earth shall be loosed in heaven")—so we loosed to him the very opposite of those things—a spirit of compassion and understanding—and thanked Jesus for hearing our prayer.

The next afternoon when Andrew came home from school he said "You'll never guess what happened in the playground today, Mum!"

"No dear, what?"

"Roger came up to me and asked if he could have a bite of my doughnut!"

"Did you give him one?" I asked eagerly.

"Not likely!" Andrew replied indignantly.

"So did he kick you then?"

"No!"

"Oh but don't you see, the Lord is beginning to work a miracle! Tomorrow take a packet of peppermints and offer him one and see what happens!"

Andrew really didn't want to do anything nice at all for his old enemy, but grudgingly agreed and the following evening at dinner his older brother Simon, who attended the senior school, said "I say, Freddie (everyone except Norman and me called him by his nickname Freddie!) Roger came up to me today and said "Hey, is that your brother over there?"

"Yes", I said. "So—what of it?"

"Oh nothing", said Roger. "But he's OK, isn't he?"

"Wow, that's fantastic!!" We were all so thrilled and relieved! Thankfully—but only with God's help—the bullying had ceased and never took place again.

Not only did the Lord do this for Andrew, but when two of our grandsons, Keith and Luke, were being bullied at their junior school and we all joined hands and similarly prayed together, they were never bullied there again.

During our years at Rosedale while working for the Children's Society Norman travelled to many places interviewing possible foster and adoptive parents, and for the most part it was a very happy experience.

I was with Norman when he handed over his very first adoptive baby, and when we met the mother we noticed she had an unusually long upper lip and chin. To our amazement, when we saw her with her new baby of a few months old, he had exactly the same facial characteristics, even though Head Office had never seen a picture of the mother. Had we not known with absolute certainty that this was an adoptive baby we would never have believed it, they were so alike!

Even though Norman knew that the people at Head Office always prayed about each case it was wonderful that in this, as in so many other cases, they obviously heard very clearly from Heaven!

It was my job to type Norman's reports, and I must admit I felt quite sorry for some of the would-be parents. I thought at times perhaps he seemed a little too strict in some of his assessments—until we came across a breakdown of a foster situation arranged by a previous social worker when we had to collect a little boy and return him to the Children's Home.

We arrived at the home of a couple in their late thirties and were shown into their sitting room. Seated in an armchair reading a picture book (upside-down) was 5 year-old Alex. He was as quiet as a mouse, but two huge tears ran down his cheeks.

"We've got all his things ready!" the foster mother told us. "And he can take the book with him." Then to little Alex: "You're going with this lady and gentleman to a home where there'll be lots of boys and girls to play with. Won't that be nice?" Alex nodded in silent anguish, and when all the paperwork was dealt with the foster parents said goodbye to him. I took his hand while Norman collected his suitcase and we settled him in the back of our car where he immediately scrambled to look for them out of the rear window.

He looked so upset, and said very sadly: "Well, they could have waved me goodbye". When I looked back the door had been firmly closed, and we had the impression that it was done with great relief. I gave him a big hug and showed him the books and games we had brought with us, but we both felt very angry that it was possible to hurt a little boy so badly. All the way to the Children's Home he kept talking about "Mummy and Daddy" he had just left.

From that moment on I was so glad Norman had such high standards, and it was to his credit that as far as we know, neither a fostering nor an adoption has ever broken down through the unsuitability of the foster or adoptive parents once he had placed a child.

There was one memorable occasion, though, when a mother desperately wanted her baby returned to her, even though she had been placed with a couple with a view to adoption. The adoptive couple were lovely; very happy together and with a keen sense of humour. They had much love to give and longed for a child of their own, yet this baby girl called Sarah, they said very sadly when they eventually had to give her back to us to take her to her mother, had never once smiled during the months she had been with them.

Although we had prayed fervently that this couple would be able to keep the little girl, it became more and more evident that her natural mother desperately wanted to keep her—and we learned afterwards that not only was her married sister having a baby but that her friend at work was also pregnant.

The upshot of this was that we had to arrange to collect the baby from Jenny and Colin and as we arrived at their comfortable home we dreaded what must have been a very traumatic parting for them. They were obviously very upset, and it was so poignant to read their note attached to the crib telling Sarah's mother how much she enjoyed playing with her teddy after her bath; her favourite baby foods, how she liked to sleep on her side and all kinds of other details lovingly included.

We stayed for a while, and they were somewhat comforted when Norman assured them that the Society would once again be placing a baby with them as soon as one became available. As we left they (and I!) were almost in tears, but even they had begun to feel that this little one would perhaps be happier with her mother. On the way home we stopped the car in a layby, as we felt very strongly we should pray for this little girl who seemed so sad. As we did, holding her fast asleep in my arms she immediately gave a deep sigh, still sleeping, and we felt sure the Lord was freeing her in some way.

We had arranged that her natural mother would collect Sarah from our home, and when we arrived at Rosedale her mummy was already there with her own mother. We hadn't met them before, but were instantly struck by their sincerity and warmth. Baby Sarah was still fast asleep, and at their request I took her into our sitting room and placed her gently on our sofa while I put the kettle on for tea.

When she eventually began to stir, her mummy, in tears of joy, took her in her arms. To our amazement Sarah instantly beamed with delight and continually smiled and cooed. When Norman contacted the family later he was told she was a very happy baby.

And what of Jenny and Colin? After several months, to their great delight, a lively baby boy was placed with them—whereupon Jenny, having understood she would never be able to have a baby of her own, became pregnant when their little Peter was only a few months old and later she gave birth to a son! They eventually emigrated to Australia where the family settled very happily.

Some of the cases were far more difficult to handle. One couple who had fostered a teenage girl for several years discovered she was stealing the mother's contraceptive pills, and her general behaviour was becoming so difficult that the foster parents, who had younger children of their own, very reluctantly decided she needed to be supervised in a Children's Home.

We had to pick her up from her school (she knew nothing of our visit) and the Headmaster promised not to ring the dinner bell until after we had collected her. Unfortunately it rang very soon afterwards, just as I went into the girls' cloakroom and was about to speak to her. I was immediately surrounded by her friends, firing questions and encouraging her to tell me in no uncertain terms and ripe language where I could go.

I managed at last to persuade her to come with me where she sat in the back of our little Morris Minor and Norman delivered her to the Children's Home, very grateful that this kind of thing didn't happen every day and only too aware of the challenge facing her social worker.

Norman's senior social worker, Julie Midgley, would come regularly to assess case histories and we would usually have a relaxed lunch in our sunny garden, especially during that hot summer of 1976. They would go through the list and together sort out any tricky problems—then pray about the children as well as would-be adoptive and foster parents.

They were golden days, but towards the end of his time with the Children's Society Norman found himself almost turning into a removals service, helping young single mums move home in places like Weston-super-Mare because they would have to move out of their summer 'lets' and find alternative accommodation, which was never easy. Although very sympathetic to their needs he always felt it was 'closing the door after the horse had bolted', wishing they hadn't chosen that particular lifestyle without the support of a husband to help father their children.

Every year in or around November Norman was invited to speak at special Toy Services in various Anglican churches where he would also collect all the toys given. These were put into our dining room, and by early December the room was bursting at the seams with all kinds of toys, books, jigsaws etc. People were always asked *not* to wrap their gifts as they all had to be checked for suitability.

We could never understand how a few of the so-called 'gifts' for these already deprived children were old, shabby and obviously unwanted; books torn or scribbled in and occasionally even broken toys. Thankfully many more were lovingly crafted: dolls prettily dressed, their wooden beds beautifully made and including all the bedding, cowboy outfits complete with hats, games still in their original wrapping and shiny new books.

Norman lovingly and meticulously chose the best presents for each individual child, and when we had wrapped and labelled them all, delivered them to the appropriate families and Children's Homes.

Chapter Six

HEALINGS AND HAUNTINGS

One morning I went to get out of bed as usual, but to my consternation felt as though my spine had somehow melted overnight and to stand up was agony. I had no idea what was wrong, but the only way I could walk was with my back arched and on tiptoe—and going to the bathroom was a nightmare! Thankfully we had no visitors at that time, but I had no idea what was wrong or how long it would last.

As soon as he realized I was in trouble Norman prayed for my healing, but nothing seemed to happen and in desperation I asked him to ring the doctor. However, he decided instead to call on Harry Greenwood, who lived just a few yards along the lane. Harry had a remarkable healing ministry, especially for back problems, and when Norman had gone to ask for his help I asked the Lord why I wasn't already healed when he prayed for me.

"How do you know you weren't healed?" came the reply. "You didn't do anything about it!"

Healings And Hauntings

It was true, I had simply stayed put when Norman prayed, so if Harry prayed for me I was determined I'd stand up somehow. In fact Harry was out but another minister at the Church, Vic Dunning, who happened to be at Harry's home at the time, came instead. After he prayed I got straight out of bed and stood up (sweating with anticipation of agony!) but to my enormous relief the pain had gone. I was able to dress and go downstairs for breakfast, so grateful for Vic's (and Norman's) prayers.

However, by the end of the afternoon the unbearable pain had returned with a vengeance and I told Norman I would have to get to the doctor somehow—but instead he called on Harry once more. This time he was home and they returned together.

"I gather you've a back problem?" he said.

"Yes, I certainly have!" I replied, "Just here . . ." but before I could tell him Harry said "Don't worry; the Lord has shown me . . ." and he put his hand exactly on the spot, just to the right of the bottom of my spine. After he prayed he told me to do something I certainly couldn't do before—touch my toes!! I had to make my mind a complete blank to even attempt it, but once again to my enormous relief the pain had completely gone.

I was puzzled. Why did pain return after prayer—with such strong evidence of healing? I asked Harry about lifting—was it OK to carry shopping bags? Should I be very careful? He explained that because my spine had dislocated even for only a short while, tendons and ligaments would take time to readjust again. Also tension can cause pain and I should *relax* when I sat, not stiffly in fear of the pain returning.

"When the Lord does a job He does it thoroughly!" said Harry. "Don't go weightlifting but just carry on normally. You'll probably ache in that area for a few days when you begin to get tired, so then just lie down and rest for half an hour or so."

I thanked him gratefully, so relieved to feel normal once again, and when over the following three days at around teatime I felt twinges in the same area I simply rested awhile until the discomfort lifted. On the third afternoon as I lay on the sofa I heard an almost audible voice snarling: "You wait, in a few years' time you'll *really* be sorry you didn't see a doctor!"

I immediately recognized the voice of the enemy, and responded: "Oh thank you Lord—You've *done* it—completely healed me!" I knew Satan wouldn't try to snatch my healing if I didn't have it already.

The next day we went to Charmouth's stony beach for a walk. I certainly couldn't have done that a few days before. Occasionally over the next year or two I would feel a twinge but always immediately say: "I bind your power over me, Satan. Thank You and praise You, Lord Jesus, for healing me!" And very thankfully have stayed free from back pain ever since.

I am so grateful for that lesson in how to keep my healing. It was such an encouragement to persevere and *never* speak negatively or confess that it hadn't really happened or it must have been a mistake—which gives our healing away and allows the enemy to infiltrate again. Proverbs 18:21 says 'Death and life are in the power of the tongue: and they that love it shall eat the fruit thereof.'

In other words, if we truly believe what we have received—it's ours to keep! Although we were quite shocked to discover that sometimes people find it easier to let healing go—until we understood one reason why.

Rosie and Edna were two ladies living at what was then called 'John Groom's Crippleage'—a horrible name we thought, now shortened to simply 'John Grooms'. Those who lived there were all disabled in some way or another, and these two sweet people came to stay over a weekend.

Rosie was in her twenties and Edna possibly in her fifties, and as always they too came along to the meetings. Both received healing, their legs having grown to the same length after prayer, and Rosie telephoned us a few weeks later, excited to tell us she bought her first pair of pretty high-heeled shoes a few days after returning to John Grooms. She also asked if they could both stay with us again, and this they did several months later.

When they arrived we were thrilled to hear that Rosie not only now had a very nice boyfriend but she had set up home in a flat and was thoroughly enjoying living an independent life for the very first time. Sadly, though, Edna was once again limping badly and we took Rosie aside and asked her how it was that she seemed to have lost her healing, which was initially so evident.

Rosie explained that for someone of Edna's age who had always lived in a protected environment it was in the end too frightening to have to face living alone and independently for the first time in her life, and since John Grooms were only allowed to support the disabled she had simply reverted back to her limp. We could well understand that at her time of life independence could have been a really traumatic experience.

What had been such an unexpected blessing before these ladies first arrived was the insistence by Norman's cousin Eric, who stayed with us only two weeks before, that he be allowed to strengthen the wooden newel post at the foot of the stairs leading up to the guest rooms on the second floor. We all tended to swing on it a little as we started up the stairs and it was beginning to work loose. We had no idea then that our next visitors would be quite so badly disabled, and had Eric not repaired it for us they might well have had a serious fall.

Later that year our near neighbours had bought an ancient Priory called St Catherine's Court near Bath, intending to turn it into a Christian conference centre. Sadly the local Council later withheld permission since the numbers anticipated using the narrow lanes could well have caused traffic accidents. But we were thrilled to be invited, along with several other friends, to stay with them for a few days and attend a big Christian conference locally. Having lived in Chard for several years we looked forward to sharing fellowship with others from different backgrounds, and gratefully accepted their kind invitation.

This was our first visit and we had no idea what to expect. As it was we arrived quite late in the evening, so it was pitch dark with just a small light over the front entrance. We could just make out a huge and very dramatic silhouette ("Golly, it looks like Dracula's castle!" commented one of the boys)—and at that time of night we had to admit it did look spooky!—but once inside Laura and Daniel, our hosts, warmly welcomed us into a huge bright stone-flagged kitchen where we were treated to supper with welcome mugs of steaming hot chocolate.

Time for bed, and Laura led us upstairs to our room on the first floor. We were very intrigued that the wide wooden staircase was built around a massive tree trunk, and this led to a huge landing which doubled as a library. We were escorted from there down a corridor to a room at the very end. Laura threw open the door to a pale beech panelled room with a built-in wardrobe and twin beds, both with warm orange candlewick bedspreads.

"This is the oldest part of the Priory, over 900 years—but you needn't worry, it isn't haunted!" she said, smiling and wishing us a good night.

However, as she left and we stepped across the threshold we looked at one another in consternation. The only way we could describe how the room felt was malevolent—evil and menacing. There was definitely a hostile spiritual entity! Our bathroom was only next door, but neither of us had enough courage to leave our open bedroom door and begin to get ready for bed until the other had returned, with great relief and "Oh, thank goodness you're back!" to comforting hugs.

Thankfully the boys' room felt quite normal, and having seen them safely settled we returned to our own.

The first thing we did was remove the bedside table and push our beds together in case we needed to clutch each other if things became even scarier! Next, we prayed *HARD*, thanking the Lord for His protection, claiming the precious Blood of Jesus over the boys and ourselves, and binding the power of Satan to cause us any hurt or harm while we were there.

By then it must have been about midnight, and when we were ready for bed Norman (at 6'3" tall!) had to stand on a chair to pull the curtains across the windows (set in incredibly thick walls) to shut out the brilliant moonlight. However, the darkness felt absolutely suffocating so after a few minutes he decided to pull them back again.

When at last we turned out the light, as usual within a few minutes Norman was deep in slumber. I snuggled into my pillow, almost asleep when suddenly there was an enormous POP! in my ear, the one on the pillow. It was so loud I saw stars just for a moment, and although I had never before experienced anything so weird I was too tired to do anything except hope nothing else would happen. I turned over, this time facing the windows, the moon shining brightly into the room.

After a few minutes, again almost asleep, I unmistakeably saw a dark shadow moving across my closed eyes, just as I would if someone had walked past in strong sunlight. This was definitely not my imagination. By now I was so tired I was well past scared, just really angry, and in a stage-whisper so as not to wake Norman I sat up, rebuked the enemy for all I was worth, bound his demonic power to stop me from the sleep I needed and prayed in tongues.

This time at last I fell asleep with no more interruptions, but I was glad when morning came. The only thing I couldn't do all night, for some reason, was stick my feet out of bed—I just couldn't!

And we didn't know until the next morning that our room overlooked the graveyard!

Another thing we didn't know until much later was that when there was a burglary a few years before, our bedroom was the only room in the Priory where police dogs refused to cross the threshold, searching for a suspected intruder.

My sister Jill, who had always said she never believed in anything supernatural whatsoever, good or evil, turned pale when she knew we had actually slept there. She and her husband Peter, with their two young children, were renting one of the Priory gatehouses while their new home in Wiltshire was being built.

It was the occupant of the other gatehouse who told them about the police dogs. They also told her that at some time a monk had burned to death in that room; inevitably terrible things could have happened over so many centuries.

Jill told us that after being shown around by our friends and commenting on what a beautiful and interesting place it was, as she stood on the threshold of our room she felt as though someone had thrown a bucket of freezing water over her. For weeks afterwards she said she daren't look up at those windows overlooking her kitchen in case she saw something horrible.

During our stay at the Priory we prayed in our bedroom for a short while every morning and by the time we left we were thankful to God that it felt very different. We are so grateful for the weapons of warfare He has given us, and only the previous year I had had prayers of deliverance from a dreadful fear I had had since childhood and never mentioned to anyone, even Norman until then—fear of one day finding myself in a haunted house!! If it hadn't been for those prayers I'd have fled screaming and gladly slept on the stone-flagged kitchen floor!

Instead, although we would never in a hundred years have volunteered for that experience, it showed us that nothing evil in the supernatural has the power to harm us when we belong to the Lord—He, by the power of His precious blood, is our shield and protection against *all* the power of the enemy of our souls. "And they overcame him (Satan) by the blood of the Lamb . . ." (Revelation 12:11)

NORMAN
1930-2008
. . . whose faith, love and integrity is his
lasting legacy

The author with her three sons and families celebrating a special birthday . . .

. . . all except Keith, our first
grandchild who was ill in hospital

Auntie Mill and Uncle Sid—
they spent their lives serving others

The Manor House

Rosedale

Summerhouse

St Catherine's Court, near Bath

Babbacombe Villa Hotel

Molly's mother—taken in
Australia after her healing

Chapter Seven

DREAMS AND DISASTER

We had been living in Chard for about three years when my sister Jill telephoned from their home in Cronulla near Sydney, Australia, to tell us that she and her husband Peter would be bringing their two children, Laura and Adam, over to England and would be looking to buy a home here. We were thrilled, and so glad we had plenty of room for them at Rosedale. They stayed with us for six months, and during that time were able to look for just the right home while Peter began work at Seaton in Devon, at what was then Racal Electronics.

In the meantime Jill asked me if it was possible to borrow enough money to put a deposit on a small car, since it would have been difficult for Peter to travel to Seaton every day without one. Although we hadn't a great deal of savings I knew Norman would be only too pleased to help out and went into his office near the kitchen to ask him. However, to my surprise he hesitated for a few moments.

"It would only be until their money arrives from Australia," I explained reassuringly.

"It's not that", he responded. "The fact is we just don't have the money to lend them."

"Whatever do you mean?" I felt as though I had suddenly been hit with a brick.

"It's the stock market. There was a huge fall a couple of weeks ago, and almost all our savings have gone!" was the reply. "Even Dad's gilt-edged shares (Norman's inheritance) have almost disappeared."

We had Andrew's school fees to pay as well as all the usual household expenses, and I just felt faint. It was such a shock it took a few moments to sink in. He must have seen my face turn white and put his arms around me to comfort me, saying, "I'm so sorry darling—I was waiting for the right moment to break the news, I know it's a huge blow. I'd love to have helped Jill and Peter. I hope there'll be some way for them to find the money for a car—perhaps a Bank loan . . ."

I was too stunned to cry then, that would come later, but it was the beginning of a time of enormous stress when a small thing like a broken window would almost send me into hysterics. It must have been an incredibly anxious time for Norman too, but he had such faith in his Lord he was a rock to us all—I was the only one who panicked.

However hard we tried to economise, though, money sometimes became frighteningly tight and I dreaded walking past our bank in case the manager saw me. I imagined him wagging a finger in admonishment because we owed money—the first time in our lives we had ever been in debt, we had always saved for whatever was needed. Sadly at that time we hadn't yet learned the wisdom of giving tithes (one-tenth of our income) to our faithful God, and we had only just enough to cover Andrew's school fees until the end of term.

The hardest thing of all was realizing, as we did eventually, that we would have to sell Rosedale. We always imagined living there indefinitely, and to be truthful I really thought God must be punishing us for something we had done wrong but I didn't know what it was. We didn't breathe a word to a soul about our predicament, but at times when cash was very scarce the Lord would send someone with a surprise meal for us all, or enough money to be able to buy food or other essentials.

As the Word says, 'I have been young, and now am old; yet I have not seen the righteous forsaken, nor his seed begging bread' (Psalm 37:25) Even so it was a period of great anxiety, and when we did eventually find a property it was incredibly hard to leave our lovely home.

I remember walking through the house, every room filled with dear memories, determined that never again would I allow a home to wind itself so deeply around my heart and wondering for the umpteenth time why the Lord had allowed us this to happen to us anyway. It was very difficult to comprehend in the light of all the hospitality we had happily given to so many people; we just wanted to serve Him as best we could. It was a real test of faith.

Little did we know then that this was all in God's plan to bless us, and that ahead of us was one of the most challenging yet exciting times of our lives. In the meantime Peter was able, thankfully, to buy his much-needed car and the family settled at Westbury in Wiltshire after their stay in the gatehouse at St Catherine's Court.

At about the time of their move Andrew suddenly discovered we had a squatter in our summerhouse. He came racing into the kitchen very perturbed, telling us he had seen an old lady sitting on a bucket smoking a cigarette, an old mattress on the floor. This really set alarm bells ringing—she could set herself on fire lighting up in a wooden summerhouse—so, giving her time to 'collect herself', we confronted her, telling her it was impossible for her to stay there, she must take her belongings and leave.

We couldn't help feeling very sorry for her. Apparently she and her husband had been moved into a care home but in separate rooms, very traumatic for them both. Having been together for so many years she found this unbearable, and had simply upped and left, sleeping rough under hedges or wherever she could find a space. Our summerhouse must have seemed a luxury.

We felt obliged to telephone the authorities since they had no idea what had happened to her, and we promised to reiterate to them her longing simply to be with her husband in their new home. She promised to leave and we gave her enough money to buy food and shelter for another night, but a few days later we discovered the door of our log store locked and guessed it must be our uninvited guest.

Once again we remonstrated with her before she left with her belongings, but you can imagine my alarm when a few days later I saw her yet again scurrying past our kitchen window, bent low to try to avoid being recognized. This time we felt we had no choice, and telephoned the police who could then make sure she stayed where she could be cared for properly while awaiting the double room now promised for the couple.

For some unknown reason though, during those few weeks it seemed as though everything gradually descended into chaos and whatever we attempted to do our hands were somehow tied. Then one morning Norman shared a very strange dream he had that night—that he awoke to see two tiny men like elves dressed in green on the threshold of our bedroom, jumping up and down with glee. Norman felt very angry that these uninvited creatures were in our house and pointed to them with authority, saying "Get *out*, in the Name of Jesus!"

Immediately they looked terrified and the next moment disappeared. He very seldom remembered dreams, but this one made quite an impact.

You can imagine my astonishment when a few days later, driving Andrew to his school in Taunton, he told me of a strange dream *he* had the previous night.

"I was in bed, Mum, and these funny little men like goblins all dressed in green were all in my bedroom, opening my cupboards and drawers and settling themselves in. I told them to go away and stop messing about with my belongings, but they said they'd only go if I went and took hold of my father's right hand. So I looked for Dad everywhere and found him in the garden and just grabbed hold of his hand. Then I went upstairs again. This time they all looked very fed up and were packing their little suitcases—so they meant to stay a long time!"

I didn't tell Andrew about Norman's dream and he hadn't mentioned it to anyone but me, but alarm bells rang and we knew this must be much more than a coincidence. Life hadn't been the same for a couple of months, every day like stepping through treacle, including the episode with our little old lady squatter and a number of other incidents that just didn't add up.

When I told Norman about Andrew's dream, like me he could scarcely believe it but knew it must be significant, and that evening we had a word with Uncle Sid.

"Well, isn't our Lord wonderful?" he said. "He's confirmed to two people in your family that things have been going on spiritually that need dealing with. You must go home and pray in every room—ask the Lord how and pray accordingly!"

When we returned home we did just that (spirits of confusion, among other things) and knew with certainty when we had finished that the oppression had lifted. Gone were the unnatural obstacles and confusion, and life thankfully returned to normal again.

'Normal' now included Norman's growing travelling ministry in many fellowships and churches around the country. Among those he was invited to minister at was a house fellowship attached to St Andrew's Church in Chorleywood, Hertfordshire. For several months a great friend, Pat Keeffe, had offered to stay with our boys if I wanted to travel with Norman at weekends, and at last I realised I was meant to do just that, and was so grateful for the opportunity.

This particular house meeting was very special in that the Lord moved sovereignly in one young woman's life with a transforming healing.

It was the end of the meeting and most people had left. Norman was talking to a man on his right, and I was sitting next to him chatting to a young woman on my left. Suddenly Norman leaned over and turned to this young woman beside me, saying: "The Lord has just spoken to me. He says that whatever you ask of Him, He will give you".

The young woman smiled her thanks and a short while later stood up to leave. We saw for the first time that she had a very pronounced limp; one leg was much shorter than the other and she was wearing a built up shoe and, if I remember rightly, calipers. (Norman said later that he wondered nervously if he should have asked if she'd like prayer, but decided not!).

However, she telephoned a few days later to tell us that the following morning she was sitting in her kitchen waiting for the kettle to boil when she suddenly remembered what Norman had said the previous evening. Stretching them out, "Oh Lord" she said, "I would love my legs to be the same length!"

With that, the short leg grew and in seconds both legs *were* the same length! You can imagine how incredibly life changing this was, and she told us with great joy that she had just been out to buy her very first pair of pretty shoes! To those who have never seen legs grow this must seem incredibly far-fetched, but we had seen this happen on a number of occasions including when it happened to me, when Derek Prince, a highly respected Bible teacher, prayed for a number of us when he visited South Chard. We do have an amazing God!

Another wonderful miracle we witnessed was at Cromer in Norfolk. We were invited by our friends Derek and Audrey Aldridge to stay for a weekend to minister at their fellowship, and when everyone else had gone home at the end of the last meeting on Sunday morning were asked to pray for Maggie, a young woman in her twenties.

She told us she was due to have her sixth heart operation shortly, but she believed NOW was the time God was going to heal her. She looked very ill and thin, her face ashen and her lips slightly blue, dark circles under her eyes. She could walk only a few yards before stopping to rest, and had to lie on her bed every afternoon.

We knew we had another appointment later that day so had little time to spare, and prayed quite a brief prayer asking the Lord to touch Maggie by the power of His Holy Spirit and heal her, though we had no idea then that she had been born with a hole in her heart.

A few weeks later Audrey telephoned to tell us that to her consternation Maggie had asked her only a few days later to accompany her to the sea, since she had always wanted to learn to swim. Since this was March on the bitterly cold east coast Audrey was very alarmed, but Maggie, with her great faith, insisted that God had healed her and this was something she was determined to do.

To Audrey's joy and relief, Maggie had not only survived the shock of the icy water but also learned to swim a width in the local pool *underwater!* She also learned to ride a bike—something else she had always longed to do—and was cycling all over Cromer telling everyone who knew her that God had healed her! To be able to swim so powerfully holding her breath when she had been so desperately ill must have been proof to many unbelievers of a complete healing for this lovely young woman, and she gave all the glory to her precious Saviour. "For with God nothing shall be impossible" (Luke 1:37)

The following year we returned to Cromer once more, and by the end of the weekend ministry were very disappointed not to have met Maggie again—we just wanted to tell her how delighted we were that God had transformed her life. However, to our great surprise Audrey said that Maggie had been at every meeting, and pointed to the corner of the room where several people were gathered.

"Come along, let me take you to her!" Audrey led the way, but as we grew nearer we were so disappointed; we were sure there must have been a misunderstanding and didn't recognize any of the young women chatting together.

"Maggie!" called Audrey. "Norman and Molly especially wanted to see you before they go home!"

When we looked again at this bonny suntanned young woman with her rosy cheeks and sparkling eyes, we were certain we had never met her before. It was only when she spoke and we heard her attractive slight lisp that we recognized Maggie. She looked a totally different person from the one we had last seen, and told us with a huge smile that she and her husband were adopting a baby and she was making up for all the time she had been unwell!

We praised the Lord all the way home!

Often we discovered that when people needed prayer for sickness, we needed to pray first for deliverance since the Lord wants to make his children whole, as well as healing them. Many times rejection, unforgiveness and fear were the culprits, and once any deep-seated spiritual problems were dealt with it could prove life changing.

One very unusual deliverance happened during a time of ministry when an attractive dark-haired woman in her forties asked for prayer after a meeting when everyone else had gone home. She needed healing, but said one of her major problems was intense anger that she found very difficult to control.

As we began to pray she confessed her anger to the Lord, told Him she repented of it and renounced it. We began to pray for her, as always in the Name of Jesus, then watched in astonishment as muscles in her slender upper arms expanded to such an extent her blouse sleeves looked as though they would split, and at the same time black hair appeared on her upper lip! If we hadn't seen this for ourselves we wouldn't have believed it, but as we prayed for deliverance from not only anger and rage but also a masculine spirit she was wonderfully set free, then healed and returned home radiant.

Deliverance is never a sought-after ministry—and we certainly didn't volunteer for it!—but knowing what an enormous blessing it is (I was so grateful for the prayers I received) it's a great joy to see the victims of enemy oppression set free at last.

When the Lord does a sovereign work it's always even more of a blessing, and when we were invited by a Canadian pastor to minister at an Anglican church in Waterlooville, Quebec he sent us copies of the posters for the event. To our consternation they had advertised it as a healing conference; we had certainly seen the Lord heal but would never have presumed to say we majored in that that particular ministry, and prayed nervously but fervently that Jesus would heal people even before the meeting!

We were staying in St Lawrence with friends who arranged for John Hill, their colleague, to drive us there and when we arrived a number of people were already gathered in a large hall. We were invited to sit on a small platform, and after a few minutes saw John in the congregation listening to his watch. To our surprise he then lifted his neighbour's wrist to listen to *his* watch and we made a note to remember to ask at the end of the meeting why he did that.

The Lord was so good to us that evening, and it was immensely comforting to be reminded that we can neither succeed nor fail when we pray—*He* is the only Source of

Divine power, and quite a number were healed and set free, by the grace of God.

When we called in at the local Dairy Maid for a late night hot chocolate John explained that he had been hard of hearing for several years, knowing he would eventually become profoundly deaf. As he sat in the hall he said he suddenly began to hear many more sounds than usual. When he removed his hearing aids he knew he wasn't able to hear his watch ticking—until he put it to his ear! He wanted to confirm that it wasn't just his own watch so he grabbed his neighbour's to listen—and could hear it clearly.

He was really thrilled (and so were we!) that his hearing had been totally restored, and we praised the Lord for so wonderfully answering prayer from weeks before and many miles away.

Chapter Eight

HALLELUJAH ANYWAY!

The next step in God's plan for our lives began with the dreaded move from our lovely and much-loved family home to a chalet bungalow a short distance away.

From the moment we moved in I really hated the place, although Norman almost swooned with joy as he pointed out the damp course. (Rosedale had none—as lovely as it was, toadstools grew in our attic rooms in the winter, and damp came downwards, sideways and upwards—we always seemed to have our hands in our pockets paying for damp prevention).

On the very traumatic removal day itself two kind friends, Pat and Diana, came to help us move in and we really appreciated their support and encouragement. That weekend happened to be Mothering Sunday, and Andrew asked if he could have his pocket money and go shopping. When he returned he had bought us both a present—for his Dad a beautifully painted glass mug and mine a pretty miniature cup and saucer. I read the little verse on it:

"My Kitchen Prayer:
Bless my little Kitchen, Lord,
I love its every nook *(I really hated our new kitchen!)*
And bless me as I do my work,
Wash pots and pans and cook"

I promptly burst into tears, much to Andrew's alarm, but I immediately gave him a huge hug of thanks and explained that they were tears of joy for my very first happy memory in our new home. We were very touched—and although sadly Norman's glass mug eventually broke, wherever we go the cup and saucer remains on our kitchen windowsill.

In reality, our new kitchen was quite spacious but hideous—an ancient sink unit and a few worktops, none of which matched, with an imitation dark oak Fablon strip behind the gas boiler (we later discovered it wasn't hiding anything ominous after all and presumed that for some strange reason the previous owners must have thought it attractive).

Potatoes were growing in the front garden below the kitchen windows and almost every shrub and flowering plant had been removed from both front and back gardens, but they had generously left us a rusty old bed frame in the centre of the back link fence where they must have grown their runner beans, ruining the lovely view of the fields behind it.

Added to that, the back 'garden' was just a huge heap of earth which the previous owners used as a vegetable allotment, and I would stand in front of the large picture window in the sitting room sure that the said heap was about to fall into the room, muttering under my breath: "I *hate* this place!" And I did.

The L-shaped hall and landing were unbelievably ugly: papered in pampas design, one strip the right way up, the next upside down, and so on, and two long walls were black with green and orange splodges. The previous owners were obviously very heavy smokers, the stained sitting room walls outlining white shapes of ornamental flying ducks while the ceiling, too, was a darkish shade of caramel. Beyond this it had no character whatsoever, and I found it incredibly depressing. In contrast to Rosedale it felt as spacious as a dog kennel.

A few weeks after moving in we began to notice, from time to time, a very fishy smell on the stairs. It was so persistent that at last we even took up the stair carpet thinking we might find the remains of an elderly kipper, but there was nothing there.

It was only then that we remembered we hadn't given the place a 'spiritual spring clean' yet, so we promptly decided to pray all around the house in every room, asking the Lord what was there. He showed us that there were occult and unclean spirits, meanness and poverty, and we laid hands on the walls and asked for the blood of Jesus to cleanse the whole place throughout.

Not only did we never encounter the awful smell again, but also my own attitude changed completely—and immediately. It was as though blinkers had been taken from my eyes and I could see at last what a lovely home we could have. All the unhappiness and resentment vanished, and I told the Lord how sorry I was for being horribly ungrateful—we were so blessed to have a roof over our heads. I thanked and praised Him, and as I did so I began to see how we could add colour and beauty, not only in the home but the garden too.

By the time we finished decorating, we had one of the prettiest homes we had ever had: soft green carpet throughout, and in the sitting room Norman made low white fitted bookshelves and a display alcove. White wallpaper sprigged with tiny pink roses matched our ancient but cosy rose velvet three-piece suite. There was plenty of room in the long kitchen for lots of pine units and a dining area, and good friends appeared unexpectedly to help us turn the lump of earth at the back of the house into a lawn.

I felt very ashamed of my ingratitude when I looked back, although we didn't realise then why the Lord had allowed what seemed to me at the time a severe punishment for something I didn't know we had done—the reason why we had to move from Rosedale. God had other plans!

A few months before our move Norman was offered another post, this time in Winchester because the Children's Society were centralizing their services and living in Chard would no longer be an option. Winchester is a beautiful city and the job sounded very interesting, but Norman knew he must be sure to make the right decision. It was difficult because the boys were all well settled in their schools and we knew we didn't want to leave our Church and so many lovely friends.

Over the previous few years Norman had been praying for the Lord to open up an opportunity to travel in ministry; on several occasions there had even been prophecies for him to that effect, but always including "Do not go ahead of Me but wait—I will show you the right time". After much heartfelt prayer he felt certain that the time had come at last, and knew he had to 'burn his boats' and prepare to trust the Lord completely, and so it was that in July 1977 he made the decision to leave the Society and began to make plans for more ministry contacts.

During that summer Duncan had been trying desperately to find work in or near Chard, which he found impossible. His speciality is radio communications, and we were so proud of him when he passed the very tough City & Guilds Radio Amateurs exam even before he took his O levels. While at school he joined Somerset Fire Brigade as a part time fireman, and then worked on military radios at Racal in Seaton, later moving to the Home Office in London. It was very sad that he had to leave home, but he did well and for the past 22 years has run his own electronics business.

Towards the end of our time in Rosedale I knew I was being challenged. If Norman was going into full time ministry depending entirely on the Lord for financial provision, I knew I needed to be certain He would provide all our household needs, too. So I thought I would begin by challenging myself to believe He could supernaturally supply eggs. Just eggs. But as the week went on and no eggs appeared I gave in and simply bought a dozen.

Afterwards I admitted that subconsciously I had known I could just go out and buy a box, so I knew *I'd* failed that test. However, the very next day another guest arrived—with a dozen of the biggest eggs I think we had ever seen! I felt the Lord say, "if only you'd waited just that bit longer!"

This was such an encouragement, and a few weeks later I was determined I wouldn't give way this time—I would trust God to provide whatever we needed even when our pantry was empty. Although I knew we had money to buy food, when I prayed about it I felt the Lord telling me it was time I really put my faith in Him. I knew there must be no cheating either—we wouldn't mention it to *anyone.*

It was Friday afternoon and apart from bread, all I had left, surprise surprise, were eggs! When the boys arrived home from school I offered a choice of boiled, poached, scrambled or fried. Only Simon chose a boiled egg, and I warned him we had no butter, only margarine which he hated. Like his brothers though, when I explained to them what I was doing they understood, despite being very hungry after school.

I had just cooked the eggs when there was a ring at the doorbell—not the usual time for a call, and I had no idea who it might be. Lo and behold!—there on the doorstep was Rosemary Andrews once more—this time with a shopping trolley full of everything we needed, and exactly on time for our meal—butter, sugar, tea, fruit, vegetables and other delights!

She explained that she had just done her weekly shopping when the Lord told her to bring it to us instead. This must have taken a great deal of grace as well as obedience, since she would have to do all her own grocery shopping again. We were reminded of that verse in Philippians 4:19: 'But my God shall supply all your need according to His riches in glory in Christ Jesus'.

I gave her a big hug (again!) and explained what had happened. We were all so grateful to her and thrilled at how the Lord had provided at the exact moment it was needed. It finally confirmed to us that when the time came our needs would be met, come what may. Norman and I (and our family) were being prepared for another new season of our lives and it was only later that we realised taking care of a very large house like Rosedale would have been a heavy burden as life became increasingly busy.

Norman had already begun visiting fellowship groups in this country, but a great deal needed to be done in the new house. For several weeks after leaving the Children's Society he worked very hard, concentrating on painting and decorating; also engaging a builder to make a front porch and open up the spacious attic. There was even room for two more eventual bedrooms and a bathroom, though we only had funds for the porch and one more essential bedroom.

By Christmas our new home was transformed, and miraculously somehow it was as though Norman was still earning a salary—we had no idea how, but for those three months before his travelling ministry began in earnest there was always money available for everything we needed.

A decision to begin a travelling ministry is certainly not one to be taken lightly, and it was on the understanding that although South Chard Church would send us out and support us in prayer, we would need to rely on the Lord for *all* our provision (and we made up our minds at the same time we would never, *ever* mention or give even the tiniest hint of any financial need—it would be cheating!). Over the following months as doors opened up in this country we also learned to look only to our Lord Jesus, never to a particular church or fellowship to supply our financial needs.

In the early days of our travels we ministered at one huge Pentecostal church in the Midlands almost continuously from Friday evening until Sunday evening. Many people received healing and deliverance, and the pastors told the congregation at the last service there would be a collection 'especially for Norman and Molly'.

We watched in amazement the congregation's generous love gifts fluttering into the offering baskets, knowing they must have given hundreds of pounds. However, on the way home we opened the envelope given to us just before we left and the cheque barely covered the cost of our petrol. It was hard to believe that Christian leaders could so deliberately mislead their brothers and sisters in Christ. Nevertheless, on many other occasions small churches and fellowships would give sacrificially and we would feel very grateful but almost guilty in accepting their generous gifts.

By now, however, our costs were rising to such an extent we knew it was time I considered going to work once more. The prospect filled me with apprehension—I had always worked as Norman's secretary, but it was over twenty years since I had been employed outside the home and I knew the style of setting out correspondence and general office work had probably changed a lot since those days.

I began by taking temping work, which was an interesting experience to say the least—and I soon realised that if there were any faulty typewriters they would always be given to the temporary typist! To my surprise, though, I really enjoyed this totally different routine, and it gave me a taste of available work.

After a few months I began to feel I would like to find a permanent post—all I needed was a place where I could take dictation (shorthand or Dictaphone), type documents and leave at 5pm—I didn't want to have to answer telephones or take on any more responsibility, life was quite full enough already.

Before we had our family I had worked in London as a secretary and one day Norman showed me an advertisement for a secretarial post in Taunton. It sounded interesting but I had absolutely no confidence whatsoever; at that time 'dolly birds' were very popular and I was a mature mum in my forties. When he pointed out that the interview itself could be valuable experience anyway I thought I had nothing to lose, so with very low expectations (certain I wouldn't get it!) I applied.

With knocking knees I found myself being interviewed for a job as secretary to the Administrative Officer which included organizing social events, typing Minutes, filtering telephone calls and general public relations work. James introduced himself and began by asking me very briefly about my past experience. To my surprise, from then on he asked many searching questions about Norman's ministry (I had to complete a form giving a few details when I first applied) and after a while I found myself telling him about our faith, miracles, being born again, baptized in water and filled with the Holy Spirit.

When I returned home having told Norman about this very unusual interview I knew I didn't stand a chance and felt very relieved, but to my astonishment (and dismay) James telephoned the next day and asked if I could begin work the following Monday. Though it boosted my confidence a little my heart sank—I'd have to answer the pesky telephone and do a great deal more than just type letters—but the salary was tempting.

However, once I'd mastered the telephone system (I kept cutting James off before he could reply!) the work proved interesting and rewarding, and only a few days after I began working there I discovered why James was so interested in our spiritual background—he was in desperate need of prayer and counselling. It transpired that as a Christian he felt utterly ashamed at giving in to his previous secretary's advances despite trying so hard to withstand the temptation, and was particularly distressed that he had betrayed his wife and family.

He would frequently finish dictation and then share his guilt and heartache, sometimes in tears. I promised that Norman and I would pray for him and his family and reassured him of God's forgiveness, especially in the light of his great remorse.

I felt there were real demonic forces at work in that secular working environment and when I asked the Lord for help, He showed me to go in early one morning before everyone arrived and pray, laying hands on the walls of our office and binding the power of the devil to cause such misery, specifically against lust, adultery, unclean and seducing spirits, afterwards loosing the love and power of our precious Holy Spirit. Afterwards there was a marked difference in the atmosphere in the office and James was clearly far more at peace.

Norman and I also prayed that the 'other woman' would move right out of the building and work elsewhere since she would often telephone at 5pm and sidle into James's office hoping I had gone, obviously continuing to chase him. It was a great relief when a few weeks later we heard she *had* changed her job at last, and some time after I left we heard that James and his family made a fresh start, moving right away from the area.

Eventually I left when we knew the time had come for me to travel more extensively with Norman. An English friend, Tony Nash, also in ministry in Florida with a thriving church in his home, had often written suggesting it would be good if Norman could travel to the United States. At the time Norman was preaching in Hertfordshire but said he felt the Lord telling him *now* was the moment to begin a wider ministry. When we arrived home a letter was waiting from Tony and his sweet wife Janet, this time saying *"When are you coming, Norm—we have plenty of room for you and Molly!"*

Chapter Nine
"TRUST IN THE LORD..."

A FEW WEEKS BEFORE Norman began his overseas ministry we were on our way to a fellowship in Godstone, Surrey, travelling along the motorway when suddenly there was an almighty bang. We had a burst tyre but thankfully were in the central lane and were able to pull over onto the hard shoulder. Norman was driving our faithful little Peugeot where the spare tyre was stored *underneath* the boot, and after trying in vain for about fifteen minutes to unscrew the spare, both praying fervently under our breath for help as he did so, Norman was suddenly aware of a pick-up truck which must have only recently parked about 20 feet behind us.

"D'you think you could ask that chap if he could give us a hand, Moll?" he said.

We were so relieved that here was someone who could help—we had a meeting in only about an hour's time—and when I approached the driver (in his thirties, I thought) he immediately responded without hesitation: "Yes, of course!" He said little but within minutes he had climbed under the boot, unscrewed the wheel (effortlessly, it seemed), jacked up the car and in record time the job was done.

We were so grateful, and I already had my chequebook ready to pay him.

"Thank you *so* much!" I exclaimed. "Now, what do we owe you?"

But he shook his head. "Nothing!" he said very firmly.

"Oh please!" I insisted. We're so grateful; I don't know what we would have done without your help!"

However, he shook his head emphatically once more, wishing us a safe journey as he returned to his truck. Norman and I smiled at one another, so thankful for his willingness to help—but turning back to wave goodbye just a few seconds later we were astonished to see in that instant both he and his truck had completely disappeared! There was absolutely no way the truck could have passed us without our seeing and hearing it.

When I had first approached the driver I thought he must have only recently come on duty since his white t-shirt and blue dungarees were immaculate. He had kind but penetrating blue eyes and fair hair, and if we had known who he was we would have asked so many questions! We were certain God had sent an angel—there could have been no other explanation.

The Word of God says 'angels are all ministering spirits sent from God to minister to them who receive salvation' . . . Hebrews 1:14. Our Heavenly Father had heard our prayers and responded in a way we could never have imagined.

When we returned home from Godstone we began to make arrangements for travelling to the States, and felt the Lord confirming that we should be there for around six weeks. We had only two prior engagements, the first at Land o' Lakes in Tampa where our friends Tony and Janet Nash lived. The second was at Indiana, Pennsylvania, where we had been invited by Stanley and Deborah Hickman to stay when they visited South Chard Church. We also, though, believed the Lord would open further doors as we trusted Him.

We had already told Simon and Andrew (Duncan was by then working in London at the Home Office) that there was no way I would go if they were unhappy about me travelling with their Dad, but they said they would rather we were together on such a long trip. We knew it wasn't an easy decision and really appreciated their loving support. They knew that if they would rather I stayed home then they would always have priority.

It was at about this time Norman was ordained by the International Gospel Fellowship, described as "a team of gifted, creative followers of Christ who serve on the 'front line' and in support roles with the purpose of making disciples among the nations by any means consistent with Scripture." It was encouraging to meet and share with others in similar situations.

"Trust In The Lord . . ."

We were extremely touched, too, by the love of Richard and Averil Norton, who gave unexpectedly and generously to encourage us in ministry.

Travel arrangements were made through our friend Pat whose sister Norma worked for British Airways, and after a few weeks, greatly encouraged by prayer and prophecy from our Church, we found ourselves at the checkout where Norma was arranging the tickets. You can imagine our astonishment and gratitude when she told us she and her husband John had been saving their tithes and felt the Lord telling them they were to pay our fares! We were so grateful for their loving generosity.

When we arrived at Kennedy Airport in New York I felt a sudden panic—"What on earth are we doing here, 7,000 miles away from our boys?" I already missed them all, and for a fleeting moment wondered if this was just a big mistake—but as I remembered the promises God had given us I felt assured that all would be well. We had to change planes for a flight to Tampa in Florida, and were most impressed with Delta airlines. It was their 50th Anniversary and every passenger was given a pack of playing cards and offered a glass of champagne in celebration.

By then we had been travelling for many hours and felt very tired, and although we normally only drank wine at weddings or other special occasions we thought it could be quite relaxing to try the champagne.

Bearing in mind we hadn't eaten for some hours it wasn't surprising that it had a fairly instantaneous effect on me—it was very nice, and I drank mine quite quickly (Norman, sensibly, wasn't in such a hurry!) Within about ten minutes I was astonished, as I turned to look at him, to see three of him and had no idea which one I should be speaking to!

Thankfully the much-needed meal came quite quickly, but I had great difficulty focusing as I tried to open the salad dressing in one of those little plastic pots. Unfortunately when I did I squeezed too hard, inadvertently showering the passenger sitting in front of me. She squirmed but didn't actually turn around, and I remember nudging Norman and whispering, "I don't care, I don't *care*!" with a giggle.

He chuckled, but looked more than a little concerned and part of me was horrified—supposing I was still tipsy as we were being met, introduced as "the minister's wife"! The other part of me unfortunately was past caring, but several cups of strong coffee soon did the trick. We didn't know then that our blood thins when flying, so alcohol kicked in far quicker than normal. I vowed never to do that again!

When at last we arrived in Tampa it was like walking into a steam laundry—and it was late evening in October! It was wonderful to see our friend Tony, who introduced us to his friend Glenn and then admitted he couldn't remember where he had put the car he had borrowed to pick us up. Cars were parked in every direction as far as the eye could see and we wondered how they would ever find it but they did, and thankfully only about fifteen minutes later we were on our way to Glenn's home.

It was stiflingly hot in the car and Tony asked Norman if he'd like his window open, which Norman said he would, with great relief, searching for the handle.

"Here you are, Norm!" Tony had removed the handle from *his* door and passed it over! It was a very old car!

When we arrived at Glenn's spacious and attractive bungalow we were given a very warm welcome by his wife Carol, and after a cup of hot chocolate were grateful for our comfortable bed. The next morning we were asked what we'd like for breakfast and I opted for 'grits'. In my youth I had read stories about the deep South, thinking grits must be crunchy and delicious.

To my great surprise (and disappointment) grits are a bit like tapioca and that first breakfast seemed quite a strange mix—crispy bacon, scrambled egg, grits (never again!) and, bizarrely, a slice of iced bun, apparently often served for breakfast and sharing the same plate! On the other hand, they were astonished that we in Britain served baked beans on slices of toast since they make the toast soggy! We had always presumed that the idea first arrived from the States.

We were so grateful for the warm welcome, hospitality and introductions given us by Tony and Janet and it made for a very interesting start to our time in Tampa where Norman had been invited to speak before several hundred adults at their Sunday School at the University Church of God. His message, centred on God's love, was very well received, and was followed by the usual morning service where all newcomers were given a welcoming red rose and a Bible bookmark.

Later we were invited to speak at the home of a couple who farmed a citrus plantation (complete with alligators in the lake in their enormous backyard) where we were warmly welcomed once more, given a delicious deep Southern hospitality meal and later driven to our next port of call in our hosts' crushed velvet-lined Cadillac. Americans don't do things by halves—and one of the things that impressed me most was their *perfumed* toilet paper!

One of Norman's last meetings in Tampa was in a condominium (apartment) belonging to a TV weather forecaster where a spectacular sunset reflected in the water's edge was breathtaking. In their attractive apartment where about ten of us met together we were told Norman's ministry was very welcome, and at the end of the meeting several asked for prayer.

The next morning we were flying to North Carolina, to a community called Lambs Chapel, waiting in the lounge for our flight call. Before the start of Norman's ministry we had prayed for enough money to be able to leave a love-gift wherever we stayed, to cover any extra costs to our hosts. We knew now we had just enough money to cover our flight and to leave another love-gift at our next port of call—and that was all.

Once again, to my shame, I began to have doubts. Suddenly, as our flight was called, the wife of our host appeared, just in time, running across to us waving an envelope.

"Norman, I'm so sorry—this is a gift from last night for you and Molly, and I forgot all about it until just a little while ago—I was so afraid I'd missed you!"

We were so grateful and relieved as we said our goodbyes, once more reassured of the Lord's provision for us.

"Trust In The Lord . . ."

Harry Bizzell and his wife Louise pastored Lamb's Chapel, a large Christian farming community in Charlotte, North Carolina where members had settled in various homesteads. We were invited to stay in the home of a hospitable young couple, Robin and Donna, in what had once probably been a wooden slave cabin around a hundred years old. It now had a spacious living/kitchen area where a log burner kept us all snug and warm on what were very cold and frosty evenings at the end of warm sunny days; there were also two bedrooms and a bathroom, where we were greeted by a tiny field mouse in the middle of the night!

There were fly screens everywhere, and as we unpacked suitcases in our comfortable bedroom with its cool white lawn curtains we could hear the incessant chirruping of hundreds of crickets while suddenly at intervals from across the fields cow hands would yell "HallelUUUUyah! Praise the LAWD!" at the tops of their voices!

Later Norman taught at a service in a large wooden barn filled with worshippers where talented pianist Kittie Sue's fingers positively flew across the keys accompanying guitars, drums and other instruments playing lively hillbilly-style choruses—it was joyous and memorable!

Over the next few days we were privileged to share fellowship with a number of families living in the community who were all generous in their welcome and hospitality. It was so fascinating to learn how they came to be there and to see the huge conference pavilion they were building in the woods; hearing stories of the generosity of local businesses who gave their skills and materials to help complete the work—real answers to prayer.

On that first night back in the cabin at about 3am in the morning, however, we both awoke at the same moment, a choking fear seeming to have filled that little bedroom. We knew if slaves had lived there they could have been subjected to all kinds of abuse, and we prayed, binding the fear and claiming the verse which says "God has not given us the spirit of fear, but of power, and of love and of a sound mind" (2 Tim 1:7) A deep peace filled the room and we slept soundly until morning.

After another few days we travelled to Atlanta, Georgia where, while staying with Tony, we had been invited to spend some time with Andrew Culverwell, the talented singer/songwriter from South Chard who now lived in a beautiful home there with his wife Sue and their children. Andrew met us from the airport and as we drove along the highway we couldn't help noticing the huge billboards announcing boldly 'PRAY FOR ATLANTA'. Goodness, how wonderful, we thought. We wished we could have that kind of Christian publicity in Britain.

However, there was a sinister reason behind this. Satanists had approached several cities to hold their annual convention and been turned down—until Atlanta gave permission. We were told that within three months the crime and divorce rate had risen considerably. The latter was partly because Satanists were praying fervently against Christian marriage—knowing how powerful that partnership can be.

So Atlanta really needed much prayer. It also showed how effective Christian prayer in unity can be . . . "For where two or three are gathered together in My Name, there am I in the midst of them" (Matthew 18:19,20) Undoubtedly we don't pray as often as we should, using the authority given us by Christ Jesus—"For the weapons of our warfare are not carnal, but mighty through God to the pulling down of strongholds" (2 Corinthians 10:4)

When we arrived it was quite bizarre to see a copy of the Chard & Ilminster Gazette on Andrew's coffee table in his beautiful home such a long way from Somerset! He was a real inspiration for Simon who had always watched him intently as he played the organ at South Chard, learning much from him about chords and harmony.

Whilst we were there Andrew and Sue took us to visit the Confederate Memorial Museum where the largest relief carving in the world is sited—three Presidents on their horses carved into the side of Stone Mountain. The horses' mouths alone were large enough for a man to stand in—we marvelled at the extraordinary skill of the sculptors.

Among other invitations we were also asked to speak at a Women's Aglow meeting in a gracious home where sliding doors separating two enormous living rooms were pushed back to allow space for well over a hundred people. After the praise and worship at the start of the meeting, Norman gave his message. Afterwards as he prayed he had a word of knowledge, telling the congregation that the Lord was healing someone of a lung problem.

Immediately there was a commotion at the back of the room and when we went to investigate, a young woman told us that as Norman spoke it was as though God had taken a pair of bellows and blown air into her collapsed lung. She was completely healed, praise the Lord! When they saw what had happened it was encouragement to others to come forward for prayer, and many were blessed that day.

Another high spot of our stay was a visit to the Reverend Charles Stanley's First Baptist Church. We watched him on TV before going to worship there with many hundreds of others at one of several services that Sunday, and I always appreciate his ministry now on one of the God channels.

It was a memorable and happy visit, and Andrew Culverwell's music is still blessing many people.

From Atlanta we travelled to Bethlehem, Pennsylvania, where we stayed with a couple in their very English style home—Joye had met Conrad during the war and become a GI bride. They and their family were involved in a thriving fellowship, and while we were with them Joye took us to Lancaster County near to where the Amish had settled, and also to meet a group of Mennonites who had built a life-size model of the Ark of the Covenant following exact Biblical instructions—except that the gold was paint, of course!

We had always imagined the veil of the Temple to be made of quite delicate fabric but the Mennonites had commissioned skilled Jewish women to weave the veil in the exact pattern of that time, and we were astonished to discover that it was, in fact, woven like very thick tweed in beautiful blue, purple and scarlet.

We were told it was so strong that pairs of oxen pulling each way could not tear the fabric! "And the veil of the temple was rent in twain from the top to the bottom" (Mark 15:38) *had* to be a supernatural occurrence, and a vivid reminder that our sins are so great to such a holy God that only a curtain of that impenetrable thickness would be sufficient to separate sinners from the Holiest of Holies where the cherubim covered the Ark.

It was also a shock to see the size of the enormous basins on the courtyard outside which would have held sacrificial blood, and a salutary reminder that often literally thousands of sheep and cattle were sacrificed as atonement for sin. How wonderful that Jesus was able to set us free from the huge burden of sacrifices as He, our wonderful Saviour, gave Himself once and for all, dying that terrible death on Calvary because He loves us so much—and for the joy that was set before Him! (Hebrews 12:2)

The Mennonites always wonder how the Chief Priest ever got through into the Holiest of Holies, since they had never discovered an entrance which didn't involve him in either crawling underneath (very undignified) or trying to squeeze in sideways, because the rings which held the curtain and covering of the Ark in place allowed so little space. They still wonder if it could have been through transubstantiation!

Bethlehem in Pennsylvania is an industrial town, yet at Christmastime becomes very beautiful; residents light a white candle to put in every window, and the whole place seems to glow. It was another visit we would never forget.

Our next stop was Indiana, Pennsylvania where we had been invited to stay with Stan and Deborah Hickman, and by the time we reached Pittsburgh Airport from where we were to depart our names were being called over the Tannoy. There were no trolleys available and by the time we reached the check-in on the far side of the airport with our heavy bags we were hot and exhausted—and very surprised to be asked how much each of *us* weighed, as well as our bags!

The man taking our details seemed very relaxed in his blue cardigan (no jacket) and then to our amazement he simply pulled aside a curtain covering a door and ushered us through. There on the tarmac was a tiny Piper 8-seater airplane—no wonder he had to check our weight!

In fact we were the only passengers and it seemed incongruous to be able to chat to the pilot, still wearing his blue cardigan. Of course the flight was totally different from the usual jumbo jet and we had wonderful views of the countryside as he pointed to various landmarks, including the crick (creek) below as we neared Indiana, landing in a quiet spot near the small customs shed with its frilly gingham curtains (not quite like Gatwick or Heathrow!).

Stan met us and drove us through the busy freeways to his home alongside other typical Pennsylvanian white painted clapboard houses nestling in a gentle valley, where his wife Deborah made us very welcome.

The previous evening I had missed the boys even more and said so, but as Norman pointed out we couldn't call from a public callbox (we'd need too many nickels) and we felt it would be a liberty to ask our hosts to make a long distance call. We prayed for the boys as always, but as I awoke next morning these strange words were ringing in my ears: "Give me your fruit, give Me your fruit, give Me your fruit, for I AM the husbandman".

I didn't understand the words at all. "If that's really you, Lord" I said, "could you please say it again?" And once more in my mind I could hear the same words but I still had no idea what they could mean. When Norman woke I told him what the Lord had said.

"What do you make of it?" I asked, puzzled. Norman thought for a moment, then said: "Well, what *is* your fruit? The fruit of your womb are our boys. The Lord is telling you *He* is the husbandman—He is taking care of them so we don't have to worry!"

That was such a comfort (though I would still love to have been able to just pick up the 'phone to hear their voices).

Deborah had made us a very welcome cup of tea after our arrival when Stan emerged from his office. "Norman and Molly, there's a telephone call for you!" We looked at each other mystified. "But no one knows where we are!" we said. "Well, the call is definitely for you!" When we picked up the 'phone, to our astonishment and delight our sons were at the other end of the line, assuring us that they were fine, we weren't to worry. "This call is at the church's expense, so talk as long as you want to!" said Stan.

We were so grateful; that conversation really put our minds at rest. But how did Stan know we had such a longing to speak to our boys? He had met them on their visit to South Chard, and simply said, "I really felt you must have missed your family and would love to hear from them". I don't know if he ever realised quite how much that loving act meant to us both.

Stan's church, called The Potter's House, was warm and welcoming and Norman enjoyed ministering at the lively services there. We were invited to the wedding of a couple in the congregation an hour or two after our arrival, and it was so interesting; Stan conducted the service wearing a white suit while his wife Deborah (a trained opera singer) sang a beautiful solo. The bridesmaids, including the tiny flower girl, preceded the bride down the aisle and later in the service the couple lit two candles. The third, already lit, represented Jesus, the Light of the World. The reception was a lovely opportunity to meet informally with many church members.

Norman was also invited to speak at a special meeting at the local Sheraton Hotel where we all gathered in a large room that unexpectedly adjoined a dinner party next door celebrating the occult Halloween. We had seen the settings—everything black, candles, table napkins, tablecloths—and many people in weird costumes. In contrast the church had invited many children that afternoon to a "Meet Jesus" party so they could have a wholesome Christian celebration and take their own party treats to share with their friends at school.

It wasn't until after Norman's ministry there that Stan told us a of church member listening to his teaching who had problems which were causing real difficulties within the church, and apparently Norman had unwittingly spoken almost exactly along the lines of what was happening. This had caused Stan real concern during the message since that member may well have assumed that Stan had betrayed his confidence, but thankfully instead we were told later that the Lord had used the whole situation to bring reconciliation.

"Trust In The Lord . . ."

After a few sunny and busy days there we flew back to Florida, this time to Orlando where we had been invited to stay with an English couple, David and Kathie Walters and their little daughter Faith. Once more we were made very welcome and soon introduced to the church David founded called The Vineyard.

After Norman's ministry there on Sunday a young man named Carl came forward to speak to David, asking him if Norman and I had ever been to Disney World. It transpired that since a tonsil operation when Carl was only five years old he had never been able to sing as a result of scar tissue that had formed. However, during Norman's message (no one prayed for him) he found to his great joy that he was able to sing once more—he was completely healed simply through hearing the Word of God!

He was so thrilled he offered us free tickets for Disney World and since we could only spare one day David and Kathie were able to list the best events. We had a wonderful time, feeling like a couple of teenagers playing truant, so grateful for Carl's generosity. He told us that he worked in an underground 'city' beneath Disney World, and how strict the working conditions were—everything had to be kept spotlessly clean and customers were always right!

After a hair-raising ride through Space Mountain ("Never again!" we said, exceedingly pale as we staggered from the little capsule after hurtling through dark space where the twists and turns ended suddenly in a sheer vertical drop!) we discovered the Hall of Presidents where we felt absurdly patriotic as with our hands on our hearts we sang "America, America!"

One of the highlights of the day was sitting for a remarkable silhouetted portrait of us both together. These gifted artists CUT our profiles (no drawing first) then dipped them in black ink and placed one on top of the other, amazingly good likenesses and all completed within about half an hour.

It would take far too long to tell everything, but by the end of the day we felt exhausted but exhilarated too. We had had a wonderful, totally unexpected treat and a day we would never forget.

The flight home was from Miami, and we were warned to take great care of our hand luggage since thieves carried empty carcasses of suitcases, placed them over those they intended to take and walked off with the lot. Thankfully we returned home safely, so glad to see our family again.

It was an amazing end to an incredible journey during which God had supplied everything we needed. It was the first of many, and we wanted to share this one (not to boast—it was not of our doing!) but simply to show what a wonderful path the Lord can lead us in if only we will allow Him. Left to our own devices we could never have begun to imagine the amazing life *He* had intended for us; so different from the future we would have planned without Him. Looking back, disappointing and even disastrous circumstances in our lives were turned to the greatest good—only He is able to do that.

Chapter Ten

YOU MUST BE JOKING!

Norman had been in the ministry for around ten years in all when an Easter conference in the Midlands where he was invited to teach had to be cancelled suddenly when the organiser was taken ill.

Unexpectedly we both felt intense relief; we were very tired and had been working for so long non-stop. A friend had recently mentioned a guest house in Malmesbury where ministers and their families were welcomed, and although Easter was only a few days away and we doubted they would have space at that stage, to our great joy and relief they had a room available. There was no official charge, but we could leave a love-gift to help cover costs of food, electricity etc.

Their ministry to us was memorable. We would never forget their unconditional love and care and the warm hospitality and fellowship around their log fire in the evening with our hosts and other guests.

Norman very reluctantly felt it was nearing the time to limit his travelling and think about our future; he had made so many trips around England, the States, Canada (several times as a guest on a Christian television programme there called 'This Is Your Day') and Israel, where he led a number of tours.

On our way home from Malmesbury we both felt our time with these lovely people had awakened a great longing to open our home once more as we had at Rosedale where people could come and find inner healing and rest. We thought perhaps we could take a big step of faith and find a property with a few more bedrooms for guests. This time though we knew we would reluctantly need to make a charge to cover our costs. As we looked into it more deeply, however, it soon became evident that unless we could find a property with at least seven letting rooms it would be difficult to make a proper living.

We began our search a few months later, beginning in Dorset, then Hampshire, Devon, South and North Cornwall, and it was intriguing to see the properties on offer but it became increasingly obvious that we would need a far larger property than we first thought.

Eventually we came to the conclusion that to make a viable living we would have to consider at least 9 or 10 bedrooms—and my immediate reaction was "You must be joking!" Bed and breakfast was one thing—half board (also providing evening meals) for at least nine months of the year was quite another.

We had obviously prayed ***a lot*** and sought the Lord—this was such a major step to take and although hospitality had been a way of life for us, this was quite a different matter since neither of us had any formal training in hotel management—and guests would be paying for their stay. The implications were quite terrifying at first—and our bank manager needed convincing that it would be a good investment!

There were an enormous number of properties to explore and it was fascinating to see the huge variety of hotels and guesthouses on offer. We were horrified that occasionally a hotel kitchen would be without any windows—stifling in the summer, the busiest time of year. In fact, even though the one we eventually chose had large windows and an extractor fan, in the height of summer with the use of the ovens, hot cupboard, hot water still and deep fat fryer it was so intensely hot I would have to go outside, sit on the step and put my head between my knees to stop fainting!

At one memorable address we shuddered at the number of dead flies on windowsills in the garden room and awful lilac nylon sheets (with beds still left unmade by lunchtime in mid-season). The proprietor kept a parrot on their feather-strewn kitchen worktop (goodness knows what Health & Safety would have made of that!) and a terrible smell from the dishwasher that they had unwisely opened to show us. At the same time we saw some really beautiful hotels, but they were just not in the right place or at the right price.

Then one day Norman, still travelling in ministry and having visited many possible properties during his travels, said he had the strongest feeling that this time he was going to find the right one. Sure enough, when he arrived home he handed me the particulars of a place called Babbacombe Villa Hotel in Babbacombe, Torquay.

He had arranged another visit there for us both on the following Saturday, and reading the details it sounded very attractive. It was on two floors only (we had seen some with several flights of stairs—incredibly hard work!) with its own car park and only a few minutes' walk from the cliff top. There would be nine letting bedrooms plus one for us which would have to be our combined office, bedroom and sitting room.

We were introduced to the owners, an elderly lady and her daughter. They ran it through a very short season from May to the end of August, but we knew we would need to open between at least Easter and the end of September—or even later. We also knew we had found the right property.

However, although this property had apparently been on the market for over a year, as soon as we came along and made an offer, someone else popped up and gazumped us. This happened twice more, and after the second gazumping (we knew it had to be the last—we couldn't offer any more) I was beginning to despair, since our home had sold and we had to move out on 20th December. I had visions of us all ending up in a grotty seaside flat somewhere over Christmas if this fell through and then we would have to start searching all over again.

The next morning as I prepared to go to work as usual (in the office of Bob and Valerie Winyard who had a cassette copying ministry near Chard) I started the car and, completely out of character, pressed the 'play' button on our tape recorder. I had no idea what was in there and we seldom listened to the radio or tapes unless we were on a motorway, but suddenly there was singing, with the words from the first chapter of Joshua: "Every place on which your foot shall tread I have given it to you . . . No man shall be able to stand before you, I will be with you . . . Be strong and courageous, do not tremble, nor be afraid, for the Lord your God is with you wherever you go!"

I had tears in my eyes as I turned the car around, rang our doorbell and said, "Norman, you've got to hear this, it's for *us!*" As we listened for the first time to this lovely Christ for the Nations song we knew the Lord was comforting us, that all would be well—and we did indeed move into Babbacombe Villa as we had hoped in mid-December. It was really wonderful to be able to have all the family together (including my Mum and Eileen) for a truly memorable Christmas!

There was room for a huge garlanded tree in the high ceilinged lounge and of course plenty of bedrooms and even space for us all to enjoy our turkey and trimmings in the large dining room, despite having many of our belongings there as yet unpacked.

It was difficult for us to understand why it had to take so many months to find Babbacombe Villa—until we realised that almost every hotel we visited taught us another facet of the trade—for instance, what proportion of our prospective income we would need to spend on advertising. We were told of the benefit of attending Trade Fairs to make invaluable contacts, and discovered how to choose the equipment needed. There were many different makes, but

Norman kept all the hotel details and pointed out that the most popular ones mentioned would probably be the best.

We also learned the best way to serve coffee and tea after the evening meal, discovering guests would whisper shyly to each other if Norman or I served them, but if we left the tray in the lounge someone would have to volunteer to be 'mother' and guests got to know one another far more quickly.

We knew we needed to decorate internally as the owners seemed besotted with blue. Much as we like that colour this was cold and overpowering on ceilings, and every door was dark blue. The hall walls were papered in huge, rather ugly flowers but there was a lovely deep crimson carpet on the stairs with matching runners on the landing that we later extended throughout the hall. An enormous lounge led into the dining room and kitchen, and inlaid into a rustic brick wall there were attractive stained glass windows which we later found very useful when we wanted to check on what was happening in the lounge!

The bedroom lighting left a lot to be desired, and before we opened we replaced the awful strip lights over beds with prettier double shades and the single hall light with a warm chandelier. Eventually we papered the hall in white satin stripe with contrasting deep burgundy doors, numbered with tiny porcelain plates which were individually painted for us in floral designs from the local Babbacombe Pottery.

We also needed central heating (there was only one powerful electric heater in the lounge but nothing else) and one gem

You Must Be Joking!

of a man came and did the whole job with no fuss within a couple of weeks. It worked perfectly.

When a hotel is sold it includes most of the fixtures and fittings, so the enormous airing cupboard was full of substantial white linen bedding, blankets and almost everything we would need. Though all was quite adequate we would like to have replaced some of the furniture and the kitchen needed much updating.

With Christmas over we had to begin preparations for opening sometime around Easter, since we were already receiving requests for accommodation. Torquay is well served by shops catering especially for hoteliers and we visited the largest in the hope of getting advice as well as equipment. The manager, a kind and knowledgeable older man, came to see what we needed and advise us on where to put everything.

We already had two electric cookers (we brought our fan oven with us) and a six-slice toaster. One complete wall was shelved and contained neat rows of teapots, jugs, bowls, cups and saucers, but we would need to buy a deep fat fryer, a hot water still (needed on tap especially at breakfast), an electric slicer (for joints of meat etc), and eventually a microwave cooker—I soon discovered that reheating sauces on a ring resulted in dark lumps—not nice.

The only other essential was a commercial dishwasher in the washing-up room leading out of the kitchen. This was an amazing piece of equipment; in only three minutes a tray full of dirty dishes or cutlery was thoroughly washed and then dried. We loved it!

Everything but the dishwasher was delivered only a few days later, and I was faced then with the prospect of having to decide what we were going to give our guests to eat. You already know about my problems with cooking, and whenever I tried to think of meals I got as far as 'roast beef, roast lamb . . . er..' and that was it.

Almost in despair one day, with the opening looming in the next few weeks, I asked the Lord to give me not only an ability to cook but also a real love for it, otherwise this was going to be like penal servitude—hundreds of breakfasts and dinners for many months every year. Half an hour later I was able to sit down and think coherently (for the first time in my life) about food! Why hadn't I prayed that prayer years ago—Norman could have been spared much uninspired cooking!

In the middle of February (having only recently sent them our change of address) we were astonished when our neighbours from Chestnut Close in London asked if they could stay with us for a few days, followed by several sales reps planning to attend a Trade Fair in Torquay. The bedrooms were ready for occupation but our dining room wasn't yet habitable, so we placed appropriate tables and chairs in the spacious lounge for breakfast; our guests had requested only bed and breakfast and we certainly weren't ready to serve evening meals.

I will never forget that first breakfast. None of them had any idea that we were not even properly open for business (let alone that they were our very first guests!) but I was so nervous and quaking when cooking their full English breakfasts with sausage, bacon, hash browns and tomatoes, I very nearly dropped the first fried egg on the floor!

I learned, over the next weeks, not to put a fried egg anywhere near fried bread or it could sabotage the egg, causing it to leak as it sat in the hot cupboard—then I'd have to cook another and find a clean plate. I discovered, too, that although men were very happy with a slice of fried bread cut in two, ladies would usually leave half of their slice unless it was all cut into quarters!

We learned very early, too, about coping with unexpected events when one of those very first visitors drank so much wine he slept too heavily and, very ashamedly, apologised profusely the next morning as he admitted wetting the bed, gave us two of the oil paintings he was selling at the Fair and offered to pay for a new mattress.

A few weeks after we moved in our friend Pat Keeffe paid us a quick visit and when we showed her around the hotel she promised to return later that month and stay for a meal. The next time, however, as she walked into the hall she said, "What have you done? It feels so different."

"Nothing!" we replied. "You can see for yourself, we haven't had time to do any decorating yet." Then we went through into the kitchen to make tea. After a few moments she said again, "Something has happened here—it feels so different. What have you done?"

Suddenly we remembered. Norman and I had admitted to each other after the first week or two that neither of us felt at all at ease going upstairs at night—it felt very spooky in an area at the top—and realised that we needed to pray throughout the hotel. After all, we had no idea what kind of people had stayed there. Once we had done this there were no more problems, and during the next seven years we would always try to remember to pray in rooms where there had been very critical or strange guests—a spiritual spring clean ready for the next occupants!

During the weeks before our official opening (and without a computer) we would be up until the early hours of the morning coping with office work, replying to enquiries, sending brochures and arranging advertising.

We should have employed staff at the very beginning but time was so limited and we were so exhausted it didn't dawn on us that we could simply telephone a "Wanted" advertisement for a waitress and chambermaid in the local paper. Saturdays, change over days, were always incredibly hard work, and we were so grateful for Andrew's help. He was taking his A levels at College in Torquay and able to use a single bedroom in winter but the poor chap was downgraded to the garage during the summer. How we would have managed without him during those first weeks I shudder to think.

We always set up for breakfast immediately after the evening meal and at about 9pm would take tea, coffee or hot chocolate into the lounge for guests' bedtime drinks. During their stay we would try to sit with all our guests in turn, having had our own meal at about 8pm. It was surprising how quickly we learned to nod off for a few precious minutes on our office chairs—no room for armchairs in our office/bedroom.

You Must Be Joking!

Up at 6.30, initially we would take tea to our guests on request (after a few weeks we put tea/coffee trays in their rooms) then while I cooked breakfast Norman would give a short Bible study in the lounge which many guests greatly appreciated—but no captive audience, it was always strictly voluntary! Some clergy valued a complete rest and break while others were delighted when Norman asked if they would like to share a message with the group.

After breakfast we would set up tables for the evening meal which I would then prepare for the next hour or more, then we made/changed beds, cleaned sinks, furniture, bathroom and toilets, vacuumed carpets and dismantled or set up bunk beds to/from the attic ready for the next arrivals.

We almost always managed to finish just before our first guests arrived at 2.30pm and our Saturday lunchtime treat was a takeaway from Babbacombe's delicious fish and chips restaurant. Looking back we wonder how we ever did it—we were so dog tired we must have looked like a couple of pandas with black rings under our eyes—and when our first lovely staff joined us it was almost like being on holiday!

As our guests arrived on Saturday I would have a pen and pad ready in case there were special dietary needs, and one elderly Yorkshire couple, Mr. & Mrs. B, assured me that they ate anything and everything—no problem. However, next morning when we still had no staff but, thankfully, Andrew had come to help over the weekend, Norman was waiting at table and came back to the kitchen with Mr. B's plate.

"Mr. B says he doesn't like tomatoes!" said Norman. "For goodness' sake, why didn't he just give it to his *wife*?" I hissed, removing the tomato and giving him an extra portion of baked beans. Norman shrugged, equally mystified, and took it back to their table. A few minutes later, "Er . . . Mrs. B says she can't eat poached egg!" he said, a little hesitantly, handing me her plate.

Can't eat poached egg?!" I hissed once more, through gritted teeth. "Then why the blue blazes didn't she say so *before*!" I took hold of the offending egg, and to Andrew's astonishment it just missed his nose as it hurtled towards the fridge and landed in the sink. I was so tired I was almost beside myself and that was just about the last straw. Norman returned from the dining room saying, "I'm ever so sorry, Moll, but table number five don't like egg." Then hurriedly: "And they don't like tomatoes—or baked beans—or bacon—or toast!!"

I looked at him in disbelief, then realised he was kidding. We all burst out laughing, very relieved that while we always played music in the dining room no one could hear what was happening in the kitchen! I still have the breakfast sheet for one memorable week when every single person at all eight tables wanted something different. That was a nightmare, thankfully never repeated.

We bought a set of matching dinner and side plates, cups and saucers, and by then I really thought my fingers were used to handling hot dishes, but to my horror just before serving dinner one evening I dropped twelve red-hot dinner plates on the kitchen floor. Incredibly only a couple smashed completely and another couple were chipped, but I found big tears rolling down my cheeks from shock. Simon, staying for the weekend, put his arm around me and whispered comfortingly, "Don't worry Mum, it's all right, really—no one in the dining room knows what's happening while the music's playing!"

On arrival day, from the beginning we always served roast beef with all the trimmings followed by chocolate pudding with chocolate sauce, and guests who came a little cautiously, wondering what to expect, looked happily pink and replete by the end of the meal, assured that they certainly weren't going to starve!

We usually included soup, and I liked to use a garnish. When serving tomato soup it was topped with a swirl of cream and a sprig of parsley in the centre, and during that first week when Norman saw what I was doing he thought he'd help, tossing the parsley sprigs casually on top. They promptly sank, leaving stalks which looked very comical—for all the world like tiny snorkels—and we had a quiet giggle as we washed and replaced them all—carefully this time!

I also had great difficulty in keeping those first roast meats hot, and although we were told we could keep meals warm for up to two hours in the hot cupboard the first attempt just caused the meat to crisp and turn up at the edges. "Try putting gravy on first", someone else suggested. When I did the gravy, too, dried up around the edge and looked horrible.

"Oh Lord!" I cried, "You've got to help me here—how on earth can I keep all this meat hot without ruining it?"

Within the hour my prayer was answered when a couple unexpectedly rang our doorbell. They ran the Christian Alliance Holiday Centre where we had met them a few weeks earlier and I was so thrilled to see them I could scarcely wait to ask how they reheated their meat. "Easy", they replied. "Just put the slices in a roasting tin at the bottom of the hot cupboard, pour boiling water over them and cover with tinfoil. You can leave them there safely for about two hours and then use the liquid in your gravy, it's delicious!"

And from then on—hopefully—it was!

The Lord helped us in so many ways, especially during those first few months at the hotel, and we both agreed that it was quite sad when we gained confidence and didn't need to rely on Him quite so constantly. Twice a week I made five large plate pies at a time, either meat or fruit, and if I was working in the little washing-up room just outside the kitchen lost in thought, it was though He nudged me when it was time to take the pies out of the oven. I only dragged my feet once, and they almost burned.

We found a wonderful butcher who telephoned every week and delivered the order. I would cook fifteen pounds of meat (5lb each of beef, lamb and minced beef) all at the same time, then slice the chilled joints into packs of five portions to put into the freezer. The wholesalers also delivered our vegetables frozen and we were advised to buy potatoes already peeled (in packs of 5lbs) because the red soil in that part of Devon permanently stained everything.

One of the guests' favourite meals was minced beef, well flavoured and wrapped in golden puff pastry scored across the top, served with plenty of vegetables. One of the nicest desserts was christened 'Duncan's Delight'. I had been mixing fruit with whipped cream on meringue bases but it was quite rich and Duncan suggested including orange sorbet as a contrast. I thought that was a great idea, so drizzled Chocolate Ice Magic (sets very fast) on the base of the meringue, covered it with mandarin segments, then a little whipped cream and lastly a scoop of orange sorbet with Ice Magic drizzled over it.

Because I didn't want to waste all the leftover edges from Saturday's huge chocolate sponge, I made individual trifles later in the week with blackcurrant jelly soaking into the sponge in individual dessert dishes. When cold this was covered with chocolate blancmange; then cream was drizzled over, chocolate strands shaken across and a fresh strawberry in the centre.

One evening I had just opened a new container of chocolate strands and inevitably some fell on to the worktop. To my astonishment (and horror!) one of the chocolate strands got up and walked away!! We ditched the container, of course, but never discovered if any of our guests had seen a few more strands that evening wandering across their dessert. (And we certainly didn't ask!)

Our deep fat fryer was a wonderful invention, and I would parboil potatoes then finish them in the fryer. They are delicious that way—crisp and crunchy on the outside, soft and fluffy on the inside. For breakfast I occasionally cooked sausages and hash browns that way too, but had to be careful to drain them well.

The fryer had to be kept very clean, of course, and had a plug that drained the fat through into an old tin for disposal. I was very short of time one morning and once I had cleaned everything made the huge mistake of forgetting to put the plug in before pouring in a substantial amount of new oil. We weren't able to clear it all off the floor before the evening meal, and spent much time skidding on layers of newspaper whilst trying to serve dinner. It's a mistake I would never make twice!

We eventually found ourselves a very experienced and cheerful chambermaid, Iris Chappell (but she liked to be known as Chi) who came down from the bedrooms one day very concerned that there were hundreds of tiny pale grey mites that had somehow infiltrated into a bedroom through the ceiling, covering an area above the window and sink. When I saw them I was equally concerned and washed them all off, smearing Polyfilla into every tiny crack, but within a very short time there were more.

So I telephoned the Council's Infestation Department for advice, and when I confirmed there was a bird's nest just outside the window they told me to buy a particular insect killer in a flat plastic shell and push it well into the nest.

"It won't hurt the birds, but will kill all the mites" he assured us.

I later relayed this to Chi who insisted on climbing out of the window herself so I held on to her tightly and she pushed the shell as far into the nest as she could. That did the trick almost immediately, and when we checked later that day it had solved the problem.

However, that wasn't the end of the story. The following May, almost exactly a year later, Norman and I were chatting in the kitchen wondering if we should buy another shell to put in the nest in case there were more mites this season. About fifteen minutes later we heard a bang; it sounded as though passing lads had kicked a football on to the roof of our glass verandah.

I looked out of the back gate but could see no one, and then as I returned I happened to glance at the flowerbed and saw something bright yellow. It was the original shell we had placed in the nest! It was extraordinary—as though they had heard our conversation and wanted us to get the message—no more!! So they had simply tossed it out!

One Saturday morning I was upstairs putting finishing touches to the bedrooms when Norman called to tell me one of our special friends, Keren Newth had arrived with her friend Sharon, but I was in such a hurry to greet them I slipped on the top stair. Thankfully I was able to turn around to avoid damaging my spine but ended up hurtling at speed down the entire flight on just one buttock. As I landed at the foot of the stairs Norman caught and held me with great sympathy as I rubbed my very painful posterior, wincing as I did so and trying to retain what was left of my dignity!

They expressed their concern, and we soon discovered that Sharon was a physiotherapist. She said I needed frozen peas over the affected part, explaining that this would help lessen the bruise. Other guests would be arriving soon but for the moment I was able to lay on our bed on my tummy while Norman found a small pack of frozen peas for my exceedingly bruised buttock.

I was so grateful he covered me with a dressing gown, because as far as I remember that was the one and only time any guest ever knocked at the door of our private room. I had my back to it, and as I craned my neck in alarm (hoping desperately it was someone I knew well) a little old lady poked her head round the door. She was obviously a new arrival, looked very surprised and apologised for disturbing me while I was having a rest!

I was so thankful for the dressing gown and made a mental note to explain myself when we met. If she had seen me without it she would have fled altogether, wondering what kind of establishment she had booked herself into!

Growing inside our long glass verandah in summer were beautiful velvety crimson Ena Harkness rambling roses, and when the lounge windows were opened the room filled with their perfume. One afternoon I felt so weary I told Norman I needed to rest just for a little while. When I looked for him about half an hour later I was surprised to see him outside with the secateurs.

"What are you doing?" I asked, slightly perplexed. "Oh, just a bit of pruning!" he said nonchalantly.

I immediately pricked up my ears—the last time he had done any major pruning was when we were first married and with the best of intentions he had reduced every shrub and plant to a uniform 12". If our neighbours hadn't seen what was happening and rushed out to stop him, the ramblers and climbing roses would have been dealt the same treatment.

When I saw what he had done I was horrified. "You've cut all the new buds off!"

"What are you talking about?" he said, "I'm just trimming it back!"

"Trimming it back? We won't have any roses at all now—and there'll probably be no birds either!" I said, really upset.

"Oh, don't be so melodramatic!" he said calmly—and infuriatingly.

"Melodramatic? *Melodramatic?!*" By now I was absolutely incensed!

"Right!" I stalked off.

Then I went into the office and took my revenge.

Now I know emptying his waste paper basket all over his desk sounds pathetic—but he always tore everything into tiny pieces—like a human shredder, as our son Simon put it! I loved him dearly and I know he genuinely intended his 'pruning' to be helpful, but now we would have to wait *another whole year* before we had any roses.

I needed to be certain he wouldn't forget!

Chapter Eleven

NOT QUITE FAWLTY TOWERS!

I SHOULD EXPLAIN HERE that Norman confided to me when we were first married (I was 21, he was 23) that he would love to go into the ministry. We had known each other since I was 15 but he had never mentioned this before, and I felt genuine sorrow.

"I'm so sorry, darling", I said sadly, "but you've married the wrong girl."

I had to tell him there were three things I could *never* be: a minister's wife (the nightmare of all those ladies' sewing circles and jumble sales), a farmer's wife (all the mud and smells), or the owner of a guest house (my total lack of cooking skills).

We can only think God must have a great sense of humour, since the two occupations which have blessed both of us more than any other have been the ministry and hospitality!

To run a hotel wasn't even on my horizon and I would have run several miles to escape the very possibility if the Lord hadn't made it so plain that this is what we were meant to do. Thankfully farming was never contemplated!

Before we had taken on any staff and I was doing my usual sprint along the landing on a fraught Saturday morning I slipped and fell with all my weight on my instep. It was agonizing, but thankfully Andrew was there once more to help me while Norman fetched the car then drove me to the A & E at Torbay Hospital.

I found it very difficult to understand how or why this should happen, but despite my panic I knew the Lord was gently but clearly telling me to "Give thanks in all things!" There was no way I could give thanks *for* this—it was an absolute disaster, since I had great difficulty standing, let alone walking, but I knew I must simply keep thanking Him *in* the situation. 1 Thessalonians 5:18 says: "In everything give thanks; for this is the will of God in Christ Jesus concerning you".

Many times we have given thanks (sometimes through gritted teeth!) in seemingly impossible situations when we can see no solution (praising Him in faith) and the Lord has never failed us yet.

At the hospital a kind nursing sister examined my very swollen foot and told me it was possibly broken, at which I protested vehemently that it *couldn't* be broken; we had no staff yet, I had a hotel to run and 23 guests to cook dinner for that evening!

She gave a rueful chuckle as she bandaged my foot but after a moment said: "I'm really sorry, my dear—but do you know I've *always* wanted to see what it's like to work in a hotel! This would be a wonderful opportunity and I begin two weeks holiday on Monday. I'm not doing anything else this first week—do let me come and help out!"

We couldn't imagine why a busy nurse would really want to waste a whole week of her holiday waiting at tables and dealing with bedrooms, bathrooms and so on, but when we protested she actually begged us once more to let her come—we could scarcely believe it but had to admit it was a wonderful answer to prayer. Since she was very happy with the pay we offered, she agreed to arrive at eight thirty the next Monday morning. Norman and I were absolutely astonished at God's wonderful provision—and what impeccable timing!

When we returned to the hotel Norman, Andrew and I all concentrated on preparing the evening dinner. I had crutches but they were a real nuisance and kept slipping off the worktops. After half an hour or so hopping around the kitchen (and getting in the way instead of letting them get on with it) Andrew threatened (affectionately) to kick my crutches from under me if I didn't sit down! With their very practical help the evening meal and Sunday's routine went quite smoothly, and we looked forward to meeting our new waitress/chambermaid Shirley again on Monday morning.

A few weeks earlier we had arranged for a photographer to come that same morning to take pictures of the hotel for a new brochure, and the local garden centre had delivered two small trees to enhance the front entrance. I found it quicker just to hop everywhere using one crutch but of course I was a lot slower than usual.

It was becoming almost impossible to cook breakfast with so many interruptions and I found myself hop-hop-hopping through the dining room, the lounge and hall and back again every time the photographer rang the front door bell. Despite my breathless impatience he seemed to think I had all the time in the world to have leisurely debates on how to make the most of the view! By this time I was beyond caring; I just wanted him to go away.

In the meantime even though he desperately wanted to get on with the busy breakfast routine, Norman had been roped in to stand on a stepladder in the garden holding down a forsythia branch with a rake to make a scenic frame for the picture!

I was muttering sweet nothings as I hopped my way back to the kitchen for the fourth time and got as far as the dining room when to my horror there was a very strong smell of burning! I arrived in the kitchen just in the nick of time—the wall cupboard was about to go up in smoke, set alight by the toaster that had caught fire! The only thing I could do (with great difficulty on one leg) was toss it out into the garden.

Smoke had drifted throughout the dining room and lounge by this time but despite valiant attempts to wave it away several guests had already gathered in alarm, wondering if we should call the Fire Brigade.

I explained what had happened and apologised for the fact that breakfast might be a little later than usual (we had to get the tea/coffee pots on the table yet and I was still cooking) but there was overwhelming relief that a worse disaster had been avoided. A few minutes later Norman joined me, suddenly aware of the near calamity that had taken place, and followed closely by Shirley.

Several guests told us later that she had breezed into the dining room with such confidence and authority they wondered if there had been a change in management! But she was wonderfully capable and adapted to the routine very quickly. She was a joy to work with, and the only time we heard her grumble was when she wondered why people had to cut their toenails on their bedroom carpet instead of in the bathroom!

A couple of days later one of our guests returned from a trip to Brixham with a huge plastic bag. She explained that she meant to buy me a bunch of flowers but couldn't resist this enormous lobster. I thought it was dead and nearly jumped out of my skin when I saw the bag twitch. I had never tackled a lobster before and wished ardently that she had kept to the flowers, though I thanked her warmly and said I would think about her suggestion that there might be enough for tomorrow's starters.

When Shirley had finished serving the evening meal I asked her if she knew anything about cooking lobsters. When she discovered we had a huge cauldron big enough to boil it in she said it would be perfect.

"What, alive?" I said, alarmed. "Couldn't you hit it on the head or give it an anaesthetic first?" She laughed and assured me that this is what you have to do with lobster, so I'm afraid I left her to it. I was very grateful that here was someone who knew what she was doing, especially when she told me the poor thing really struggled to get out.

There was only one problem. After it was pulled to pieces and she had prised out all the flesh she said she knew there was a poison sac somewhere but wasn't sure where, and it was all in a basin in the refrigerator. I had a hair appointment just after lunch and spent most of the time fretting that we could have a hotel full of very poorly guests that evening if it *was* poisoned.

Then I had a brainwave—I would call at the supermarket on the way home and buy a large tin of John West's! No one would know the difference and it would give me great peace of mind; but I hadn't the heart to tell Shirley that after all her efforts I'd played safe and thrown the original away. The guests plainly couldn't tell the difference, and I vowed never to accept a lobster again if I could help it, even if it did make a great starter.

Shirley asked all kinds of questions about the hotel, why it was called 'Christian' and what brought us there in the first place. It turned out that she was Jewish, and we had some very interesting conversations before she left for her well-earned holiday. She was such a treasure, and intrigued to learn she was a real answer to prayer!

Because I was on my feet for so many hours each day my injured foot continued to be a problem for some months, but when guests Mark and Sally Harris and their little family were returning home from their holiday with us, Sally asked about my limp. When I explained the injury she asked if I would mind if her church prayed for me.

Needless to say I was delighted, and a couple of days later a letter arrived enclosing a handkerchief. Their church in a little Somerset village called Haselbury Plucknett had prayed over it (as in Acts 19:12) and before I went to bed I wound the handkerchief around my foot and thanked the Lord for healing me. The following morning when I put my foot to the ground there was no pain at all! I was so grateful for their love and compassion and that pain has never returned, praise the Lord!

Things began looking up again a few weeks later when we eventually employed our first waitress. We interviewed several, and one particular young woman dressed in Goth style with white make-up, blue lipstick, eye shadow and black spiky hair, to say nothing of her black nail varnish, would have scared any elderly guests to death!

When Carolyn Hanlon walked through the door, however, I just scrawled a huge YES! across my clipboard—she had a sweet personality and even before she told us how experienced she was we were delighted to have found her. We discovered she was a Christian too, and her cheerful daughter Jane who was equally able, eventually joined us to help out—they made a great team, and we were so grateful for their advice.

I had no idea how to set out a cheeseboard professionally but Carolyn showed us how to make it look far more inviting simply by including grapes. She was very skilled at carrying six hot dinner plates at once and became very popular with our guests.

The only time she had a problem was when an elderly man needed his entire dinner (roast beef and all the trimmings) liquidized because of his difficulties in swallowing, and I poured it all into a large soup plate. Carolyn took one look at it, collapsed with laughter and said, "Molly, I can't take it in looking like that! It looks like a huge cow pat!" So we disguised it with gravy!

Another tip I was given was in cooking frozen vegetables, especially cauliflower, broccoli and peas. If I brought them to the full boil and switched off the heat, keeping them in the pan as long as I would normally cook them, the vegetables didn't disintegrate and looked far more attractive in the dishes.

Norma, an ample Yorkshire lady, came to help with washing up during the busy season and fitted in very well. One day she came in exhausted with a bad cough, obviously not sleeping. I was very concerned and searched through our medicine cupboard for a bottle of linctus but without success, so offered her a packet of Fisherman's Friend. She considered for a moment, then replied, "No thanks luv, I'd rather 'ave me cough!"

She and Brenda, our other chambermaid who took turns with Chi, liked to have a smoke outside before they went home. One day Norma called me to the kitchen door, pointing to the corner of the steps where there was a pile of about 20 cigarette ends which I hadn't noticed before.

"Look, Molly", she said, shocked and pointing. "Now that wasn't *me*. I wouldn't do that, I always dispose of my fag-ends properly!"

I assured her that I knew she hadn't done it and she went on to tell me news of her sister. Suddenly she finished her cigarette and, still chatting, to my consternation threw it, still very much alight, over our closed back gate. I hesitated for a moment waiting to hear a scream, fearing it could have landed on the head of some poor unsuspecting passer-by! Thankfully, when I opened the gate the pavement was empty.

She looked after her sister with great devotion for several years but after she died Norma fell ill herself, becoming quite frail. I visited whenever I could, and tucking her into bed one evening she caught hold of my hands and said, "Will you pray for me, luv? I know Jesus is with me but I'm still afraid." When I told her again how much He loved her, she said she wanted to commit her life to Christ. As we prayed together she was filled with great peace. We have such a tender Shepherd, and she went to be with Him quite soon afterwards.

Advertising Singles Weeks brought a particularly good response. Our first venture in 1986 included Anita, a lady on crutches who had a badly injured foot. She went for a short walk along Babbacombe cliff top, but after prayer from another young woman (whom she had only just met) the Lord wonderfully healed her and they were able to walk down to the beach and climb the steep hill back before returning to the hotel. We all watched in astonishment as she walked in normally, carrying her crutches! Glory to God!

Over the years we would have opportunities to pray with guests, but occasionally we would be told: "I came with a frozen shoulder/arthritic knee/in long-term pain—but now the pain has gone!" All without specific prayer—a sovereign work of our Lord Jesus.

Every day after breakfast and dinner I would visit each table to make sure all was well and checking that everything was satisfactory. One threesome, a married couple and another relative, were always quite rude whenever I stopped by their table, even though I always stood back so as not to interrupt their conversation.

They were 'passing trade' and even though Norman had already showed them our very reasonable tariff they queried it with me again when they returned, so I confirmed with Norman that yes, he had told them exactly what I had said, and they reluctantly booked themselves in for several days.

However, they continually seemed to find fault even where there was none, and about a week after they left we received a *six-page* letter of complaint from them. Their criticism was so bizarre I had to take a second look at their envelope; I was sure it was addressed to the wrong people.

In their letter they complained of "tinned meat!" We had *never* served tinned meat. They complained that we served frozen vegetables (although we always served vegetables in season there would have been very little choice if we hadn't served *some* out of season) and also that they were served cold (Carolyn had to carry a tea towel between serving dishes because they were burning hot).

They also told us they had complained to the Council's Health Department, so we weren't at all surprised when someone turned up to examine our kitchen and ask about the details in the letter. We asked him to please look in our fridge and freezers and see for himself whether anything in the letter was true.

After a lengthy examination he returned to the lounge and explained that the writer wasn't unknown to the department; he advised us to ignore the letter which was sent as usual hoping to be offered a free holiday! This was a wicked thing to do, and if we'd received it during the first year or two it could have completely destroyed our confidence.

God had many surprises for us during our time at Babbacombe, and we were so blessed by Ron Barrow, an evangelist with a remarkable gift of words of knowledge. With his wife Carole they stayed for just a few days on the way to his next ministry. After greeting us when they first arrived, he looked very directly at me and said he would like to pray for me before they returned home. I was suspicious of anyone I didn't know well and was sure I'd had all the prayer I needed while I was at Chard.

The next morning we had coffee in the lounge with them and with Pat Keeffe, who had also joined us for a few days. After a short while he turned to Pat and told her something about herself which was very encouraging and which he couldn't possibly have known unless the Lord had shown him. He then turned to Norman. He had no idea we were financially very stretched, and proceeded to tell him about a man who had similar financial difficulties and how God had met *every* need.

When he turned to me he said, "Come here, Molly; the Lord has shown me I must pray for you" I reluctantly stepped up, convinced that any needs I had were dealt with already, but as he held my hands and began to pray I fell under the power of the Holy Spirit. For what seemed like an hour I simply cried—initially like a small child and eventually great sobs, and when I attempted to get up he said, "The Lord hasn't finished with you yet!" And back I went, crying yet more until suddenly I saw myself as a little child being held tightly by Jesus, my face buried in his neck and feeling totally loved and comforted.

I felt there was a tremendous healing of things that had happened in my childhood, the terror of watching my Dad, normally a kind and gentle man, turn into someone unrecognisable when he was drunk, verbally and physically attacking my mother. Later there were deep wounds from the treachery of friends we loved dearly, which was very hard to forgive without God's help. Many of us carry baggage with us of some kind that we collect through the years, needing a spiritual 'spring clean' from time to time.

It was a remarkable experience, and we were so grateful for the love and encouragement Ron and Carole brought to us. In the years following, much of their ministry was to gypsies in Eastern Europe where many came to know the Lord Jesus Christ as their Saviour.

Some of our guests were real characters, one notable example being Miss Dexter, a little lady who had been coming to Babbacombe Villa for years. She had a tiny wee dog she named 'Gelert' after a very large and courageous animal who had apparently given his life to save his master. Although we didn't normally take pets she carried him everywhere unseen in her holdall and very few guests knew he existed.

Another tiny, very slender lady with the appetite of a sparrow would apparently count her strands of All-Bran into her dish—"Usually about twenty!" Carolyn told us. She went on a coach trip one day and on the way home when she was dropped off in Babbacombe a very strong gust of wind caught her and blew her several yards up the road. She landed flat on her face, amazingly completely unhurt—while her handbag sailed in the opposite direction. When we pictured what had happened we tried very hard not to smile! A kindly neighbour saw her on the pavement and gave her a lift back to the hotel just in time for her evening meal.

Little Jimmy was another kettle of fish altogether. He arrived with his little sister Janey and their adoptive parents late one afternoon, his father having done an inadvertent hour-long detour into the Devon countryside on their way to us. After greeting them and showing them their room I made a tray of tea. The children also wanted tea, so I chose the largest pot before taking it into the lounge.

Following me five year old Jimmy trotted through the dining room to the kitchen where he demanded that they must have table seven, the one he liked best. I explained that they were in room nine so they had to have table nine and then, warning of the dangers of all the hot surfaces in the kitchen, took him by the shoulders and gently wheeled him back into the lounge.

Chatting to his parents, Gwen and Frank, I was horrified to see little Jimmy trying to pour tea from this huge heavy teapot. However, when I pointed this out they said nonchalantly "Oh that's all right, he does it at home!" His three year-old sister was standing next to him and they could both have been badly scalded.

The next morning I was in the middle of preparing breakfast when Norman came racing in.

"Quick, Molly! Where are the dust sheets? I need enough to cover the landing floor!"

"Whatever's happened?" I said in alarm.

"Jimmy set off the fire extinguisher" he said in exasperation, "and it's covered the carpet and the walls, everything's dripping wet!"

"Thank goodness it wasn't chemicals!" I thought, dashing to the airing cupboard where there were a few old sheets on the bottom shelf.

When he arrived back in the kitchen, hot and dishevelled, Norman commented that at least when it happened Jimmy's father had the presence of mind to take the extinguisher outside and let it finish emptying on the forecourt.

Later that morning when Chi went up to clean the bedrooms little Jimmy pointed to it, insisting, "It shouldn't have been there where children could touch it!" She immediately put her face very close to his and warned him: "Don't you *dare* go anywhere near it—do you understand?" She could look very severe when she wanted to, and he fled. We couldn't have placed the extinguisher anywhere else since it was too heavy to put any higher, but he was obviously repeating what his parents had unwisely said in his hearing.

Almost every day while they were with us something untoward happened. The following morning Jimmy slipped trying to climb up the shower, fell, hit his chin and split his lip and had to go to hospital where he had a couple of stitches.

On the fourth day Norma saw them walking along our quiet road, the children playing footsy in the gutter. The extremely busy Torquay Road was only a few yards ahead, and Norma called out to their parents twice in case they were unaware, but they shrugged and took no notice and the children continued playing in the even busier road. "Ee, you're a couple of b . . . idiots!" she shouted. (She didn't know they were our guests!)

On the last evening they were with us Carolyn remarked that they all seemed to have left their table very suddenly even before they had time to finish their dessert, and when I peeped through the stained glass window I could see them in the lounge. Frank especially seemed very jumpy, looking apprehensively in the direction of the dining room.

When Carolyn went to check their table Jimmy appeared to have literally bitten a lump out of his glass, the jug of water had spilled over the tablecloth and the remains from the vegetable dishes were all floating on top. They hadn't even stopped long enough to collect Janey's shoes; they were full of water under the table.

We all heaved a sigh of relief when they went home.

In the autumn of that year the Conservative Party Conference was held at The Palace Hotel only about a quarter of a mile away, but one of Mrs. Thatcher's bodyguards preferred to stay with fellow Christians and had booked in with us. He was a real James Bond type, quiet and with a very pleasant personality, but we sensed he had a backbone of steel when it was called for.

Towards the end of his stay we asked him what it was like to work for Mrs. Thatcher. He replied that he enjoyed his job, and during the years he had worked for her and through all their travels by plane, car or train he had never heard her speak ill of anyone.

We also met her cook who was very disabled and happened to be at an RAF Nursing Home at Storrington in West Sussex, where Eileen, my mother's sister, was now also being cared for. The cook had worked at Downing Street and Chequers from the time of Harold Wilson right through to Mrs. Thatcher, and during conversation we asked if she had any preference for a particular Prime Minister.

She thought for a moment and replied, "Harold Wilson I think, because he was so down to earth!" Having said that, she also added that when Mrs. Thatcher was giving a banquet at Chequers for various dignitaries, a new young waitress was serving dinner when she had an accidental spill on to a guest's lap. Mortified, she fled from the room weeping.

Mrs. Thatcher put down her napkin, ran out of the room after the little waitress, put her arm around her shoulder and said comfortingly, "My dear, you mustn't distress yourself; it could happen to anyone". We thought her concern for her staff rather than the dignitaries spoke volumes.

By the third of our seven years in the hotel Norman realised he would need another source of income before he retired—interest rates were already 11% when we began and by the time we sold seven years later had risen to a crippling 18%!! He had always loved books and wrote to SPCK (Society for the Propagation of Christian Knowledge) who had their own bookshops all over the country, asking if they had any vacancies for a rep. To his joy they had, and they were exceptionally helpful in his new venture.

They were the first of over 23 publishers whose lists he eventually represented over a huge area; he would motor many thousands of miles during his ten years of travelling. He really enjoyed his work and always said booksellers were a breed apart! He earned their trust by his honest appraisal of the suitability of the books he sold for their particular store and received many letters of appreciation when he retired.

By then we had excellent and very supportive staff, but since accounting wasn't my forte at all I was so grateful that Norman was able to take care of the accounts of not only his book sales but also the hotel. Life was extraordinarily busy for both of us and one afternoon I needed to ask his advice about bookings, taking my clipboard with me into our office/bedroom.

Norman was sitting at his bureau engrossed in figure work so I waited quietly for a few minutes when a wasp suddenly flew in through the window and made a beeline for him. Protectively I waved my clipboard fiercely at it—whereupon most of the neat piles of papers on his desk fluttered gently over the floor!

"Oh *Molly*, look what you've done—it took me nearly an hour to sort it all out—now I've got to do it all over again!"

Clearly (and understandably) very upset, he got up from his chair in exasperation and began retrieving his papers from the floor. I moved his chair away to pick up a few more, but without warning he suddenly decided to sit down. "*DON'T!*" I shouted—but too late! Of course there was nothing to sit on so I grabbed him under his armpits and tried to lower his 6'3" frame to the floor (with difficulty in such a limited space) as gently as I could.

Scrambling to his feet and by now flushed with effort and annoyance he shouted irritably: "Oh for goodness sake Molly, GO AWAY! I was getting on nicely until you came along!"

"I'm ever so sorry dear, but I was afraid you'd get stung!"

"I'd *rather* be stung than have to sort this lot out all over again!"

I crept out. And made him a nice cup of tea.

Chapter Twelve

TIME TO SAY GOODBYE

If we had any doubts about whether it was time to sell the hotel and begin our next venture they were soon dispelled when the time came for most of our wonderful staff to find work through the winter months when we were simply unable to support them financially, so they had no option but to look for permanent work. We were so sad to see them go, and appreciated them all even more when we took on two new waitresses and another new chambermaid.

Helen seemed a nice enough girl when she came for the interview. She was sixteen and although her first love was horses she needed to earn some money as an evening waitress. However, although she was quite pleasant to the guests she was seldom on time even when we pleaded with her not to be late, and when she did eventually arrive she would stand waiting for instructions, watching us tearing around preparing the evening meal as if we were some kind of free entertainment.

Almost every evening we went through the same old routine:

"Helen, are the bread rolls on the tables?" (We always hoped she'd catch on that we were in a hurry)

"Oh no . . ." and off she would go to distribute them in her leisurely way, followed inevitably by:

"Helen, are the butters there?"

"Oh no . . ." Next,

"Have you checked the cutlery?"

"Oh no . . . and lastly,

"Have you filled the water jugs?" The answer was almost always "No".

We knew if we'd asked her to go and muck out stables she'd have moved like lightning but it became intensely irritating to have to keep repeating ourselves night after night. She didn't seem to have any initiative whatsoever—although we did see her as a single mum wheeling her new baby in his pushchair a year later.

Janet came to work as an experienced morning waitress and was a good worker. The only problem after the first few days was the fact that she watched me closely, seemingly willing me to drop something or make a mistake. It was difficult to understand why, since if anyone else did so I would always say, "Don't worry, no one does these things on purpose", and we'd simply carry on. When I told Norman I think he must have thought I was becoming paranoid—until one morning when I asked Janet if table five had had their morning tea yet.

That was Janet's golden opportunity. "Oh Molly, you're *so* funny!" she said. "Don't you remember, table five went home yesterday! Oh ha! Oh haha! Hahaha!" And she went off triumphantly at last into the dining room.

Meanwhile Norman, who had witnessed this, went out of the kitchen door and on his way to the office stood making faces at the window, his thumbs in his ears, waggling his fingers and quietly chanting "Na na nanana!" He really made me laugh, but at the same time I thought, "Why should I have to put up with this woman?" It seemed I was treading on eggs every day as she longed to catch me out somehow, and I began to wish I could do without her services altogether but it was peak season and just not possible.

In my desperation I was reminded again of the weapons of warfare we had been given, so when she had gone home I prayed fervently, binding the spirit of witchcraft (controlling demon) influencing Janet, forbidding it to return, and once again loosing to her a spirit of compassion and understanding. I also prayed in the washing up room as well as the kitchen and dining room, asking Jesus to fill them with His love and peace. I was so glad I did, because after that she was so different—genuinely kind and helpful, and when eventually it was time to leave at the end of the season we were all sad—and she was actually in tears.

As the end of the season drew near we were inevitably exhausted. It wasn't only the long days, short nights and physical exertion, but mentally we always had to be ahead of time, making certain we had all the provisions we needed for the following weeks.

By the time the very last guest before Christmas had gone home and we had said our fond farewells waving them off as usual, we would grab each other and dance jubilantly around the lounge before collapsing in a heap into armchairs. We would fall asleep immediately for at least a couple of hours, knowing we had the luxury of time to relax at last.

After six years we initially had no plans to close the hotel, but the neighbouring lovely old building, originally with a thatched roof, was suddenly and unexpectedly bulldozed to the ground, to be built into flats. It was embarrassing, since we had always advertised the hotel as being "quiet and secluded"—but here we were at the beginning of the new season apologising profusely to our guests for the noise, dust and not-so-picturesque view of diggers and cranes.

When the same builder offered to buy our own hotel we didn't hesitate for very long. After seven years we felt it was time to bow out gracefully while the business was going well. We realised, too, that passing trade had noticeably reduced—a great contrast to a few years before we opened. Then the police would canvass the streets asking for people to open their home to holidaymakers newly arrived at Torquay railway station looking for somewhere to stay. Health and Safety measures had also increased to the extent that we would not only need a new commercial refrigerator at an enormous cost but also other expensive amenities.

By now, though, interest rates had soared and overheads had risen with them, and as we prayed we felt the Lord prompting us to prepare to move into a home in Babbacombe where we could welcome hotel guests who would like to stay with us again.

This led to a whole new chapter of our life where we were almost made bankrupt by a crooked solicitor—we had still not learned the wisdom of giving to and trusting God for *all* our finances—and I had breast cancer . . . but that's another story! Thankfully we had wonderfully supportive Christian neighbours, Eunice and Derrick Black, in our new 3-bedroomed 'upside-down' house with glorious views across Lyme Bay from the dining room, and where once again guests were able to stay—but only for bed and breakfast!

After seven busy years there our family found a lovely home for us in an ideal situation here in Bognor Regis where I still live very happily, much nearer to them.

Duncan and Aurora's home with their three sons, Keith, Luke and Timothy, is in London. At the time of writing this was Duncan's 22nd successful year in his electronics business—and I shall be eternally grateful for the first computer he built for us—it has revolutionised my life! Aurora is a very accomplished chef working for the Metropolitan Police in Westminster.

Simon and Sandra with young Poppy, Monty and Barty live in Felpham, just a short walk along the promenade from Bognor, and although Simon works as a stockbroker in the City of London his music continues as he regularly visits Nashville and St Louis in the USA, where he teaches at songwriting workshops. Sandra worked for a few years at Chichester Law Courts as a prosecuting barrister, but is also a gifted teacher who now home schools their children.

Andrew and Emma and their children Daisy, Bertie and Bea now live in a little Devon village near Exeter. Almost a decade ago Andrew, who also trained as a barrister, set up his polling firm in Millbank, Westminster and pops up from time to time on TV or radio. His work is fascinating and he, too, has built up a very successful business. Emma worked for a number of years as a G.P., a very caring doctor as well as daughter-in-law.

Simon and Andrew married sisters whose parents, Keith and Angela Henderson, live only a short walk away. My daughters-in-law are a great blessing too, and I am immensely grateful for the loving care and support the family have *all* given me in so many different ways, especially since my beloved Norman was called home in 2008. I shall always miss his love, companionship and great sense of humour, but the Lord did a wonderful miracle for me at the time of deepest grieving.

I truly believe that the numbness after bereavement is a gift from God to help us cope with all the practicalities. Sadly, when feelings return it can be immensely painful, and about three months after Norman died I found the physical pain of loss unbearable. I simply prayed, "Lord Jesus, You've got to do something for me; I just can't handle this pain. Please help me".

Immediately came the words spoken very tenderly: "Are you thinking more about Norman than about Me?"

"Oh . . . yes, Lord!" I suddenly realised all my thoughts had been concentrated on my husband. "Please forgive me and help me love You more!" *Immediately* it was as though His hand scooped deep inside me and took away all my unbearable grief—it was an instant miracle, and so comforting to know that although I will always miss him, I don't have to fight that intense pain any longer. I was (and am) eternally grateful.

Even so, I asked Him very wistfully one day why I couldn't have had Norman here on earth for another couple (or ten!) years, and He said very clearly: "I have a work for you to do."

I couldn't begin to imagine what work I could possibly do at my time of life, but only a few months after Norman died my sister Jill, still living in Perth, Australia, telephoned in January to say (totally unexpectedly, it was a great shock) that she was dying of cancer and would love to see me—could I buy an open ticket (which would take me to the end of May). I shall be everlastingly grateful to our generous sons who made it possible for me to go, and she was thrilled.

It would have been impossible to travel so far with Norman, whose health for some months before he died wasn't too good and the 27 hour journey door to door is exhausting—and yet I couldn't have gone without him. Jill was on morphine even before I arrived, but it wasn't until then that I realised she really couldn't cope with anyone else at home except her husband, Peter.

It must have been so hard for him to watch her suffer although she was incredibly brave, but her condition had worsened so alarmingly fast that she was very soon in the care of Silver Chain, the equivalent of our Macmillan nurses, at home.

Knowing I couldn't stay was a traumatic moment, and I really don't know what I would have done if my dear friend Eunice hadn't invited me to stay for the next six weeks—I shall always be so grateful for her kindness. Eunice lost her own husband while we were neighbours in Torquay, and since she and her family emigrated we have always missed one another.

Eunice has a spacious home in the Outback at Roleystone, about an hour's journey from Jill and Peter in Perth, where she made me very welcome. It was a blessing to meet her friends and family and be able to visit Jill weekly, thanks to Peter's kindness in ferrying me to and fro. I was so glad to be able to stay for a while, too, with their lovely daughter Laura, her husband Roger and their three children.

Jill and Peter have had a very tragic life—three of their four longed-for children died and they must have almost lost their minds with grief. Sadly Jill could never believe she would be good enough for Heaven, no matter how many times I reassured her that none of us were. The day before I said my final farewells my heart was aching as I begged the Lord to take her to be with Him when her time came, but after a while He whispered very tenderly: "Don't you know my love for her is greater than you could ever know?"

I felt great peace and thankfulness then, knowing she was going to be safe in His arms.

I was in Australia for six weeks and my dear Jill died very peacefully just three days after my return. I was so grateful to have been able to see her again this side of Heaven.

After 55 years of marriage inevitably I miss my beloved Norman every day, but I am so grateful to God for the love of family and friends. One way of coping was to look around for others needing help; in those early days it was the only way I knew how to survive. Prolonged grief can be very destructive, and while I was thinking of others there was no time for self-pity—and as soon as it raised its ugly head and I began feeling sorry for myself I knew I had to stop *immediately* and remember the many blessings I have been given so freely.

Looking back on those early days before Chard, I'm so relieved that I didn't try to persuade Norman to stay in London instead of moving to Somerset. Life would have been very different and we would have missed many of the blessings Jesus had in mind—not just for us, but for others too. I am so glad the Lord knows us far better than we know ourselves.

He showed me too that if we put anyone or anything before the Lord it hinders our walk with Him, and when He commanded us to have no other god before Him it is only because idols (false gods) have no power to help or guide us. Jesus Christ said, "I am the Way, the Truth and the Life, and no one comes to the Father but by Me" (John 14:6). And the hopeless, the helpless, the grieving, and all who put their trust in Him, their loving Saviour and Friend, find real hope and a purpose for living.

If you don't yet know Him, why not simply ask Him to forgive you for everything in the past and invite Him into your life? You will find He will be your best Friend as well as your Saviour. If you are truly sincere, your life will never be the same again—and His plans for you could be far greater than you might ever imagine . . .